Volution

A Philosophy of Reconnection

by
Peter Merry, PhD

Ubiquity
University
Publishing

Ubiquity University
Publishing

ISBN: 978-1-963036-00-8

petermerry.org

volutiontheory.net

ubiquityuniversity.org

Cover design, diagrams and content layout by Jon Cheetham Design Ltd.

joncdesign.co.uk

Dedication

This book is dedicated to those who are committed to going deep to go far, to offering new perspectives that take into account ever more of our reality and uplifting humanity in the process.

It is also dedicated to Ubiquity University, a community of people who through thick and thin have continued to build an organisation that is an example of the new kind of education needed for humanity to transition to a more life-affirming existence on this planet.

Nothing is invented, for it's written in nature first.
Originality consists of returning to the origin.

Antoni Gaudi

Table of Contents

Summary

Everything that is part of life is created out of a tension between a current and potential reality that represents a vacant niche in the ecology of life. That tension, that vacuum, exerts a pull on the unified field[1] which starts a process of giving form to the impulse that emerges out of the tension. That process, when looked at as a flow, can best be represented by the form of a torus. When looked at geometrically, it can be represented by Buckminster Fuller's jitterbug model[2] with its ongoing unfoldment and enfoldment, as consciousness expresses information holographically in energy-matter and space time.

The core motion of a torus is spinning and pulsing, which is why the term *"volution"* is so apt to describe it: *"1. a rolling or revolving motion. 2. a spiral turn. 3. a whorl of a spiral shell"*.[3] *"Volution"* is also at the core of both *"evolution"* and *"involution"*. In searching for a name to describe the process behind those two dynamics, *"volution"* serves us well.

Volution itself can be seen as a breathing process, a continual pulsing of an energetic flow of information between, on the one hand, subtler dimensions of life that most humans do not perceive consciously and, on the other hand, more defined and denser dimensions of life that humans tend to be able to see with our eyes and feel with our bodies. It describes how these various states of reality - as described for example by Wilber[4] as causal, subtle and gross - interact with each other as one dynamic whole. This process is congruent with a holographic view of reality.[5]

This theory of life has been explored already through the lens of physics.[6] Given the fundamental nature of this perspective, my interest lies in exploring how it relates to human culture and society. My thesis is that volution provides a way of looking at ourselves that can both integrate and transcend a developmental evolutionary perspective with an understanding of how we are related to all other aspects of life, in both time and space. That is why I refer to it as *"trans-linear"*.

This is a summary of the case for volution that I unfold through the book. Each chapter starts with the piece of the argument that it goes into:

Looking out at the world, we can see for every entity at every level:

i. a boundary field *("Unified Field")* created by the original impulse for the entity that transcends yet includes every part of the entity.

ii. an aspect of an entity that we can perceive with our 5 senses *("Relative Manifestation")*.

iii. and an aspect of reality that exists in between the two *("Ubiquitous Spirit")*. The Unified Field is different to the Absolute Oneness *(or "God")* in that the Unifying Field is something we perceive with our understanding and as such is always a relative part of a bigger whole, whereas Absolute Oneness is our inner subjective experience of oneness.

A tension of potentiality (a vacuum or niche) activates the co-creative process from the unified field, leading to fruition and a new integrated life form. The volutionary process is a continual flow and exchange between levels of manifestation of varying density (gross/subtle). It is holographic in nature. The journey from seed impulse to mature fruition can be described as an octave of 8 phases. The mature form (fruit) becomes the seed for the next level of the process, if there is a niche for it to respond to. It may also have fulfilled its function and just dissolve.

This volutionary perspective can be applied to human individual, cultural and societal development.

There are practices, both implemented by current communities and documented by the wisdom traditions and today's progressive scientists, that can be used to work with all dimensions of this volution process (beyond merely the part of the spectrum that most of us can analyse).

---

[1] *Lefferts (2012)*

[2] *Lefferts (2012)*

[3] *Merriam-Webster online dictionary*

[4] *Wilber (2001)*

[5] *Currivan (2017), Talbot (1991), Wilber (1982)*

[6] *e.g. Bekenstein (2003), Chown (2009), Haramein (2013), Susskind (1995)*

Endorsements

"Peter's words are like an echo, reaching into the deepest part of 'me', and resonating and echoing throughout the entire universe. May we all learn to have the same experience of Life and to communicate with each other as Peter is able to do. That will transform the human world. For good."

John Greenhalgh

"Peter Merry pushing out the boundaries of understanding reality again. Seems like this dirty-blonde Brit was born to inquire into the nature of being and bring out the playful flow of the universe in everything he touches. Rock on rabble rouser, the mechanisms of our current illusion are shaking as we collectively question the who what and why of reality."

Dr Barrett Brown

"Peter Merry has written a book for the human future. Based on the latest discoveries of physics concerning the Unified Field, combined with sacred geometry and integral anthropology, Peter has laid out an evolutionary understanding of ourselves and our world in such a brilliant way that we can live our lives aligned with the deepest truths of the larger cosmic whole."

Dr Jim Garrison

"Dr Peter Merry is a master teacher who has the ability to explain his toroidal-volution theory at a very succinct level so that everyone understands. Dr Merry states that 'everything that is part of life is created out of a tension between a current and potential reality that represents a vacant niche in the ecology of life.' He substantiates this argument with the latest research in cutting-edge science, sociology and integral philosophy.

"Volution is a must-read for anyone who wants to discover and journey into the true nature of ourselves, the world and how all enfolds in a co-creative way."

Dr Gyorgyi Szabo,
Dean of Graduate Studies at Ubiquity University

"Peter Merry has written a significant and beautifully researched theory of what he calls volution. This work is an invaluable guide which brings together many perspectives to support the reader in understanding consciousness and life itself. A wonderful contribution."

Malcolm Stern,
Co-founder "Alternatives", Psychotherapist and author

"I remember experiencing moments of timeless beauty and cosmic harmony when you were describing the essence of volution."

Joan Arnott

Language and Definitions

While writing this I often struggled to find adequate language to describe the perspective I was trying to lay out. I have sometimes used language that might be interpreted in a more limited way than it was intended. Here are a few definitions of how I use certain words.

"Consciousness" - an interior perspective of the ultimate oneness (as compared to "Unified Field" which is more of an exterior perspective of the ultimate oneness).

"I" - I as a persona, in the full knowledge that this I is not a Self that is separate from the rest of life, but just one way in which the Universe is choosing to explore itself.

"Information" - The field of things coming into form through intention, literally in-form-ation.

"Life" - an impulse of consciousness and process that seeks ever greater differentiation and interrelatedness in our Universe.

"Physical" - any information expressed as energy-matter in space-time.

"Universe" - spelt with a capital U throughout to denote my experience of it as a living entity and not just a rational scientific concept (which the word with a lower-case "u" tends to suggest).

Acknowledgements

First of all I would like to thank all those who have put their energy into making Ubiquity University and its Wisdom School exist, the only place on the planet I could find where I could do a PhD on this subject.

I would also like to thank my Major Advisor Dr Jude Currivan for taking the time and effort to patiently guide me through this dissertation process. Her original work has been an inspiration to me and being able to check my assertions with someone whose intelligence, authenticity and honesty I so respect really gave me the courage to do this. After all, I was merely intuiting these insights at the start, so to have them confirmed, deepened and developed with her has been very reassuring.

Next I'd like to thank Helen Titchen-Beeth who took the time to read through the whole manuscript and suggest changes that would make it more digestible for readers outside the academic world. Apart from her attention to detail, her assurance that it was worthy of becoming a book gave me the confidence to proceed.

Finally much love and gratitude to my wife Marcella who has had to put up with me raving fanatically about a sequence of wild theories about life, the Universe and everything over the years.

She has kept me grounded and patiently dealt with anything that slipped through the cracks at home while in my world of ideas and possibilities.

Thank you all!

The skiff of my being drowned, dissolved, entirely, in that Sea.

Then, that Sea broke up into waves, Intelligence danced back,

And launched its song,

And the Sea covered over with foam,

And from each bubble of foam something sprang, clothed in form.

Something sprang from each light-bubble, clothed in a body.

Then each bubble of body-foam received a sign from the Sea,

Melted immediately and followed the flow of its waves.

from **Suddenly a Moon Appeared** *by* **Rumi**

List of Figures

List of Tables

Introduction

Background

Ever since humanity moved from hunter-gatherer and agrarian, neolithic cyclical ways of life and into industrialisation, we have seen ourselves in the context of linear space-time.[1] This linear perspective grew in dominance and brought forth evolution theory. It fuelled our quest for growth and development, not only in the material and economic domains, but also in personal development circles, where the notion has taken root of a drive to transcend onwards and upwards beyond the limitations of our material reality.[2]

In recent years, that continual thirst for material progress has caused people to question the industrialised mindset at many levels. The ecological consequences of our on-going push for greater material comfort are being reflected in the growing alarm around climate change and related issues.[3] In self-development circles, people are realising that as our consciousness expands, we must both deepen our relationship to our bodies and resolve and release past traumas that may be withholding energy needed to fuel our further development[4] while keeping us locked in fear-based patterns of behaviour.[5] As wisdom traditions point out, inner and outer worlds reflect each other.[6]

Current linear ways of understanding the life process in science and cultural studies are inadequate to help us embrace and engage with the ecological and societal interrelationships needed to navigate the complex issues that humanity is currently facing worldwide.[7] The combination of these challenges is forcing humanity to seek out new ways of understanding ourselves, the world and life itself. Although linear developmental thinking does not accurately reflect the latest findings from the frontiers of science, for example,[8] the predominant worldviews of our own individual and collective development continue to follow linear ways of thinking.[9]

That linear developmental paradigm moves, by definition, away from earlier phases of development that relate to our physical and instinctive selves, towards more complex, abstract and refined stages. The implication in this evolutionary paradigm itself is that the goal and greater value lie in the later stages, risking a blindness to the value of the earlier stages upon which the later stages actually rest.

The Purpose of this Book

A simplistic return to pre-modern living, however, fails to honour the journey we have all made together so far.[10] My quest in this book is to identify a way of seeing ourselves, our world and the process of life that will allow us to integrate our deep precognitive felt sense of relationship with the dynamic holographic self-organising world that the new sciences are describing to us, while honouring the various insights that have been revealed to us along the way. In seeing ourselves and the wider world through this lens, I believe we will naturally start to be and act in ways that are more aligned with the life process itself, thereby increasing our chances as humanity of playing a constructive, co-creative role with all the forms of life that are part of our worlds.

Sources of Inspiration and Information

In preparing to write, I looked into three main domains:

• the need for new thinking and practice.

• integral models.

• existing volutionary perspectives.

The first domain includes literature demonstrating the need for new thinking and practice that reflect a greater sense of dynamic interrelationship. It covers the ecological challenges that our current thinking and practice have exacerbated[11] as well as broader analyses from anthropological, societal, psychological and philosophical perspectives.[12]

The second domain covers approaches that emphasise thinking and practice rooted in an assumption of wholeness and inter-relatedness. This includes works broadly categorised as integral thinking[13] as well as more process-oriented publications focusing on the practices that people can adopt once interconnectedness is assumed.[14]

The third domain consists of material that contributes directly to the volution thesis, with references to the dynamic holographic nature of life. Some works attempt an objective description of reality,[15] while others assume that reality as given, and describe practices that follow from that assumption.[16]

Together, this literature review provides the foundation for the volution thesis. The insights from the three domains are woven throughout this book to present the thesis and are not presented independent of each other.

The Main Idea

The theory of volution has been taking shape for me over a number of years. The basic hypothesis is that every part of life is created out of a tension between a current and potential reality that represents a vacant niche in the ecology of life. That tension, that vacuum, exerts a pull on the unified field[17] which starts a process of giving form to the impulse that has emerged from the tension.

That process, when looked at as a flow, can best be represented by the form of a torus. When looked at geometrically, it is best represented by Buckminster Fuller's jitterbug model[18] with its ongoing unfoldment and enfoldment, as information and consciousness combine holographically in energy and form.

The core motion of a torus is spinning and pulsing, which is why the term *"volution"* is so apt to describe it - *"1. a rolling or revolving motion. 2. a spiral turn. 3. a whorl of a spiral shell."* [19]

"Volution" is also at the core of both *"e-volution"* and *"in-volution"* In searching for a name to describe the process behind those two dynamics, *"volution"* serves us well.

Volution itself can also be seen as a breathing process, a continual pulsing of an energetic flow of information between, on the one hand, subtler dimensions of life that most humans do not perceive consciously and more defined and, on the other hand, denser dimensions of life that humans tend to be able to see with our eyes and feel with our bodies. It describes how these various states of reality - as described for example by Wilber[20] as causal, subtle and gross - interact with each other as one dynamic whole. This process is congruent with a holographic view of reality.[21]

This theory of life has been explored already through the lens of physics.[22] Given the fundamental nature of this perspective, my interest lies in exploring how it relates to human culture and society.

My thesis is that volution provides a way of looking at ourselves that can integrate yet transcend a developmental evolutionary perspective with an understanding of how we are related to all other aspects of life, in both time and space. This is what makes it *"trans-linear"*.

I am proposing that a holographic, fractal and trans-linear perspective can successfully be applied to human and cultural development.

This book represents an original philosophical argument including a comprehensive literature review, as well as reflections on my own experience in personal practice and organisational development, providing a research basis and contextual framework for the concept of volution.

The Research Approach behind this Book

The research combines three main existing research approaches. The first is Philosophical Inquiry, in which one goes in search of the most fundamental answer to a question. Each step of the way I am looking for the pattern that I can identify that lies behind the other patterns that I can see. In this approach, I map out different expressions of a volutionary perspective, review them and contemplate the pattern that connects them.

The second is the Grounded Theory method, which identifies patterns across existing data points, codifies and categorises them, and is then able to draw meta-conclusions connected to and grounded in the diversity of original findings. This enabled me to review the array of ideas and theories related to volution, identify the patterns across these, and allow an overarching picture to emerge. Seeing patterns in this way across different contexts enabled me to build the case for the holographic nature of life.

The third is Organic Inquiry,[23] which emphasises the importance of the individual's interior experience and inquiry as a source of knowledge and insight.

Many of the insights I have gained so far about volution have emerged from contemplation of thoughts I encounter and experiences I have had through my own personal development and systemic energy practices. Organic Inquiry offers a framework for including my inner experiences in my research process. I applied this by reviewing my journal entry notes around my personal practices and continuing to develop an awareness during my practices of how my experiences relate to the volution theory. Seeing these patterns in myself and connecting them to patterns around me also helped to establish the argument for a holographic perspective on reality.

The research process itself primarily involves a literature review together with an exploration of patterns in the world around me and in my interior experience. Organic Inquiry supports the experiential research, with Grounded Theory enabling the categorisation of insights and the identification of patterns that connect. Philosophical inquiry allows me to contemplate what is emerging and discover the most fundamental level of reality accessible to me.

---

[1]   *Wilber (1996)*

[2]   *Cohen (2011)*

[3]   *Lovelock (2006), Lynas (2007), Rischard (2002)*

[4]   *Wilber (2000)*

[5]   *Currivan (2011)*

[6]   *Lao Tzu, Mitchell (trans. 1999)*

[7]   *Laszlo (2001), Wheatley (1999)*

[8]   *Laszlo & Currivan (2008), Currivan (2017)*

[9]   *Beck & Cowan (1996), Wilber (1996, 2000)*

[10]   *Wilber (1996)*

[11]   *e.g. Gladwell (2002), Laszlo (2001), Lovelock (2006), Lynas (2007), McIntosh (2008), Rischard (2002)*

[12]   *e.g. Baring (2013), Calleman (2004), Grof (2012), Leviton (2007), Lippe & Schouten (2010), Macy (1998), Stewart (2000), Wilber (1996, 2003)*

[13]   *e.g. Beck & Cowan (1996), Bloom (2000), Graves (2002), Merry (2009), Whitehead (1957), Wilber (2000, 2001)*

[14]   *e.g. Artress (2006), Cohen (2011), Macy (1998), McTaggart (2011), Merry (2009), Senge et al (2004), Taegel (2010), Wheatley (1999)*

[15]   *e.g. Currivan (2011), Currivan (2017), Doczi (2005), Edmondson (2009), Haramein (2013), Hardy (2008), Jahn & Dunne (2005), Kieft (2011), Laszlo (2004), Laszlo & Currivan (2008), Lefferts (2012), Nichol (2003), Roney-Dougal (2010), Sheldrake (1981), Talbot (1991), The Three Initiates (2006)*

[16]   *e.g. Andeweg (2009, 2011), Keen (1998), Leviton (2007), Rayne (2012), Small Wright (1997), Spangler (2010), Taegel (2012)*

[17]   *Lefferts (2012)*

[18]   *Lefferts (2012)*

[19]   *Merriam-Webster online dictionary*

[20]   *Wilber (2001)*

[21]   *Currivan (2011, 2017), Talbot (1991)*

[22]   *e.g. Bekenstein (2003), Chown (2009), Haramein (2013), Susskind (1995)*

[23]   *Clements, Ettling, Jenett, & Shields (1998)*

Chapter One :
Trinity

The Thesis: *Looking out at the world, we can see for every entity at every level:*

i. *a boundary field ("Unified Field") created by the original impulse for the entity that transcends yet includes every part of the entity.*

ii. *an aspect of an entity that we can perceive with our 5 senses ("Relative Manifestation").*

iii. *and an aspect of reality that exists in between the two ("Ubiquitous Spirit").*

The Unified Field is different to the Absolute Oneness (or "God") in that the Unifying Field is something we perceive with our understanding and as such is always a relative part of a bigger whole, whereas Absolute Oneness is our inner subjective experience of oneness.

"This, then, is how the material thing becomes beautiful – by communicating in the thought (Reason, Logos) that flows from the Divine."

from the **Enneads by Plotinus**

"The Tao begat One. One begat Two. Two begat Three. And Three begat ten thousand things. The ten thousand things carry yin and embrace yang. They achieve harmony by combining these forces."

Tao Te Ching

The Trinity across different traditions			
Reference	*Container*	*Manifest*	*Dynamics*
Generic	One	Many	Between
Merry	Unified Field	Relative Manifesation	Ubiquitous Spirit
Wilber (1982, 176)	Mind	Matter	Prana
Walter Russell (Binder 1993)	One	Many	Relationship
New Science	Information	Matter	Energy
Taoism (Baring 448)	Tao	Teh	Ching
Taoism (Harvey 1997, 17)	Way of Final Reality	Way of Authentic Human Life	Way of the Universe
Christianity	Father	Child (Christ-Mary)	Mother, Spirit
Indra's Net (Buddhism)	Unmanifest godhead	Nodes	Web
Tibetan Buddhism	Dharmakaya	Nirmanakaya	Sambhogakaya
Kabbalah	Kether	Chokmah	Binah
Aurobindo	Transcendent/ Shakti	Individual/ Prakriti	Universal/ Mahashakti
Plotinus	Divine Intellect	Matter	Reason/Logos
Greek			Sophia
Nature	Banks of river		Flowing water
Yoga			Kundalini
Self-Mastery	Higher Purpose	Grow	Accept present
Jung (Baring 263)	Psychoid, Unus Mundus	Matter	Psyche
Quantum (Baring 342)			Quantum Vacuum
David Bohm	Implicate Order	Explicate Order	
Hologram	Unity of initiating beam	Split beams and recombination	Holographic image
Alchemy		King, gold	Queen, silver
Corpus	Father	Man	Cosmos
Hermeticum Currivan	Informational Membrane	Platonic geometric forms	Aether, Higgs Field, Dark Energy
Spangler	Primal Substance	Incarnational Realms	Higher Order Realms
Wilber (1982, 158)	Causal	Gross	Subtle
Ancient Egypt	Horus (Order)	Set (Chaos)	Hathor (Mother of the Universe; starry river of milky way) (Baring 75)

Table 1 : *The Trinity across Different Traditions*

Trinities exist within many religious and spiritual traditions.

The identifiable pattern underlying these trinities is reflected in the volution theory. Table 1 shows how various terms from different traditions can be matched with the three core aspects of the Trinity. Binder[1] created a similar table to describe Walter Russell's work which he called *"three basic types of words"*:

1. **ONE** words express the concept of unity, wholeness, absolutes, and absence of division into parts, and an absence of opposition. Examples include 'omnipresent', 'omnipotent' and 'omniscient'.

2. **MANY** words express the concept of individuality, diversity and the presence of opposition. Examples include 'this', 'that', 'you' and 'me'.

3. **RELATIONSHIP** words express the dividing or connecting lines that relate apparently separate parts to each other. They reconcile opposites into the harmony of rhythmic balanced interchange by linking individuality in diversity with unity and wholeness, and linking division or multiplication with a balanced whole. Examples include 'love', 'plus', 'minus', 'equals', 'force' and 'facilitate'.[2]

ONE would be the equivalent to the Container in Table 1, **MANY** to the Manifest and **RELATIONSHIP** to Dynamics.

A description of the basic Trinity follows.

The Container

Everything begins with the container, which also permeates all parts.

At the universal level, this is often referred to as the Akashic field;[3] at the level of a specific group or species, the morphogenetic field.[4] It is a membrane containing the information that shapes the entity. This container is beyond the capacity of any entity to make sense of, because it is the container within which all parts exist. Therefore it cannot be compared to anything else using the relative language of the entity whose container it is. It is like a fish being in water. The fish has no way of seeing the water within which it swims as a whole and therefore no language to describe it.

Likewise, we ourselves have no way of stepping outside the container of unity that holds us and our experience. The fact that we cannot step outside it means that we cannot look at it as an object, nor define or describe it adequately in words.

Nediodow describes the container by using the concept of information:

"Information stands for the immaterial field of reality. Matter is a manifestation of energy. Matter and energy result from immaterial information fields and are an actualisation of information. Information is thus the most fundamental principle of existence. Neither matter nor energy can exist without information, but information can exist without matter or energy." [5]

Elgin describes the container as the *"Meta-Universe"*:

"The Meta-Universe is assumed to have been present before the Big Bang and is the generative ground out of which our Universe (including the fabric of space-time) emerges in the flow of continuous creation. The Meta-Universe thus infuses, underlies, and transcends our cosmos."[6]

"Consciousness" has also been used as a descriptor, as in this quote from Max Planck, one of the originators of the quantum revolution:

"I regard consciousness as fundamental. I regard matter as derivative from consciousness. We cannot get behind consciousness. Everything that we talk about, everything that we regard as existing, postulates consciousness."[7]

The container can also be seen as the *"soul"* of the entity. The soul holds the pattern of potentiality; it is the field that is formed in that tension between manifest reality and a niche needing to be filled. It holds the higher purpose of the entity and literally in-forms it. All parts of the entity, including its experience, occur within the embrace of the soul. It is also important to remember that the development of the parts of the entity also impacts the soul or unifying field in a reciprocal relationship (more on this in Chapter 3). As Small Wright states, *"A human in form is, by definition, a soul fused with nature".*[8]

The container of an entity is different to what might be called Absolute Oneness, God or Ein Sof (Kabbalah). Because the container bounds an entity, it holds, by definition, a finite amount of information on its surface. Given that our experience of oneness knows no boundaries,

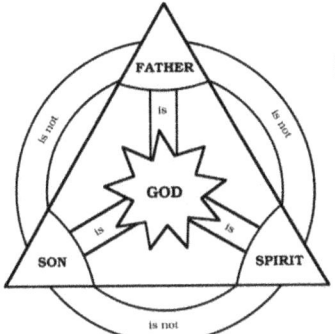

Figure 1 : *The Christian Trinity and God*

we need to distinguish between a description of unity we perceive with our understanding (a container that is a unifying field for an entity, including ourselves) and an experience of unity that by definition cannot be described in relative words by our rational intelligence. Figure 1 depicts how the Christian tradition distinguishes between the Trinity and God. Note that Father is not the same as God. The Container that I describe here would be the equivalent to the Father, not God. Ken Wilber makes the point in this way:

"Most of the great traditions - such as Nagarjuna's Madhyamika Buddhism and its Emptiness, or the Christian Cloud of Unknowing, or Vedanta's notion of nirguna Brahman, the via negativa of "not this, not that", maintain that you can't qualify ultimate reality at all (including that way), because all of our concepts are dualistic. They only make sense in terms of their opposite (e.g. infinite vs. finite, matter vs. energy, good vs. evil, one vs. many, reality vs. illusion, pleasure vs. pain) - and yet Reality has no opposite (metaphorically it is "nondual," or as the Upanishads put it, "beyond the pairs" - beyond the pairs of opposites, Bonaventure's coincidentia oppositorum)."[9]

The expression of the container is fractal and holographic, meaning the same design is reflected in all parts of the system it contains. One may not be able to describe the quality of our own unity container, however we can ascertain that there is a unity container, because we can feel it in our meditations, and we can see how that unity container shows up in other life forms, fractally, around us.

David Spangler describes it, based on his experience, as a *"primal substance"* that is *"alive, active, sentient, and generative. Whatever we call it, it differentiates and manifests itself in many ways; physical matter is the product of one such differentiation whereas the various subtle rounds represent other differentiations."*[10] His *"primal substance"* would be volution's Container, *"physical matter"* the Manifest, and *"subtle realms"* equivalent to Dynamics. It is worth quoting his description of the Container fully:

> *"At the heart of all things is a generative mystery, something indefinable and indescribable, which is the substance from which all other manifestations of matter arise. And it's important to remember that this primal substance is alive and sentient, containing the qualities and potentials that make life and consciousness as we know them possible, as well as other forms of life and consciousness that we may not yet recognise or be familiar with."*[11]

Ultimately, any description of the oneness that holds us will fall short but it is still possible to attempt to point each other towards it. Due to the fact that it escapes our rational mind, poetic language is often a more adequate way of giving us a feeling for our own unity container.

"I am dust particles in sunlight.

I am the round sun.

To the bits of dust I say, Stay.

To the sun, Keep moving.

I am morning mist, and the breathing of evening.

I am wind in the top of a grove, and surf on the cliff.

Mast, rudder, helmsman, and keel,

I am also the coral reef they founder on.

I am a tree with a trained parrot in its branches.

Silence, thought, and voice.

The musical air coming through a flute,

a spark of a stone, a flickering in metal.

Both candle and the moth crazy around it.

Rose, and the nightingale lost in the fragrance.

I am all orders of being, the circling galaxy,

the evolutionary intelligence, the lift,

and the falling away. What is, and what isn't.

You who know Jelaluddin,

You the one in all, say who I am. Say I am You."

Say I Am You *by* **Rumi**

The Manifest

The second aspect of the Trinity is the manifest reality that we can experience and measure with our five senses, that we can see and reflect upon with our rational cognition.

This is the world of objects and parts that have their own unique identity and can be compared to other parts. They seem to have boundaries we can define and qualities we can analyse. This is the world that most of us live in and take to be the norm for the large majority of the time.

This world is a reflection of our rational cognitive ability to break things down into smaller pieces and analyse those parts for their unique qualities. It is the world of the senses where we can feel and smell and taste and enjoy the wonderful pleasures this manifest world has to offer our physical bodies. It is information manifesting in space-time. It is that which is born, which is why it may be compared to the child born from the marriage of Mother and Father.

Manifest reality plays out through the duality and polarity of the Mother and Father, and their reconciliation through the co-creative potential of the Child. It is where individuation takes place, where things are a microcosm of the macrocosm.

Whereas the first aspect of the Trinity is known as the Unified Field, this is the world of the Many and the Relative. This is David Bohm's Explicate Order,[12] the visible reality, as compared to his Implicate Order, that which is invisible and yet to be born into manifestation.

These two aspects, the container of potential and that potential realised in form, can be depicted as the vesica pisces, the two core elements interlocked, as shown in Figures 2 and 3.

They hold each other in balance.

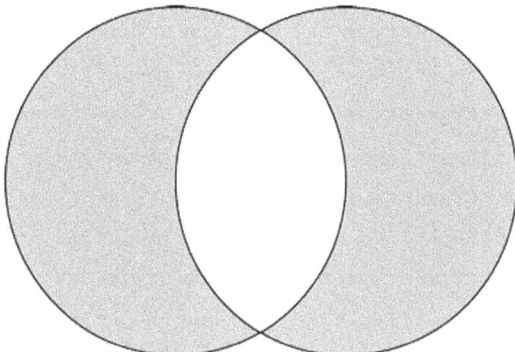

Figure 2 : *The Vesica Pisces - 2 Dimensions*

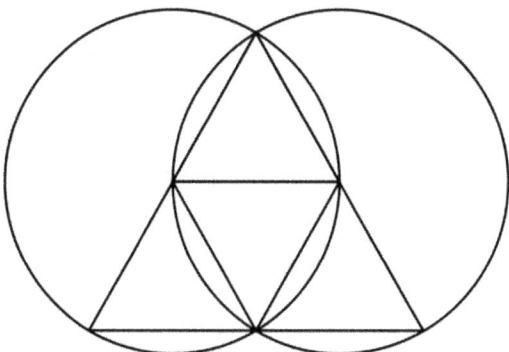

Figure 3 : *The Vesica Pisces - 3 Dimensions*

The Dynamics

The third element (shown as a triangle in Figure 3) describes what brings the dynamic tension to life, between manifest reality and potential.

This third aspect of the Trinity is the process whereby things come into manifest form out of the original impulse while being held by the unifying container. It describes the field of possibilities in potential, an energetic flow of information that is looking to become denser, more tangible forms of reality. Small Wright[13] uses 'intelligence' instead of 'information': *"Intelligence is the organising dynamic that provides the movement of soul through form"*.

This third element may be referred to as the domain of subtle energies, forms that are not yet fixed and concrete enough to be visible to our eyes in the three-dimensional world that we see around us. In Taoism the Tao is the oneness container, the Teh reflects the manifest reality and what we are considering now is the Ching of energy flow.[14] In the Christian tradition, the Father is the oneness container, the Son represents manifest reality and the Holy Spirit is the feminine equivalent to the creative force that permeates everything, and which this third aspect of the Trinity represents.

Whereas to our eyes the second aspect of manifest reality seems fairly static and fixed in its form, this third aspect is continually changing and exploring different possibilities and permutations for coming into more visible, fixed form.

In the Hopi language, a distinction is made between the *"manifested"* and the *"manifesting"*. Abram explains:

> *"The "manifested" ... is that aspect of phenomena already evident to our senses, while the "manifesting" is that which is not yet explicit, not yet present to the senses, but which is assumed to be psychologically gathering itself toward the manifestation within the depths of all sensible phenomena."*[15]

This once more illustrates a tradition that identifies the manifest together with the dynamics of manifestation in the potential.

Currivan[16] describes the ancient concept of Aether, and what she sees as its modern equivalent in the Higgs field, in a way that fits very well with this third element of the Trinity. She says that Aether *"was accepted as an all pervasive constituent of the Cosmos for two millennia - its presence perceived as underlying and breathing spirit into all physical manifestation... the Higgs Field is an ocean of energy...responsible for many of the properties of the wave/particles of matter and energy."*

Anne Baring also points to these three elements and their interaction:

> *"The physical Universe's continued expansion carries with it an inbuilt template of information that apparently existed from its very beginning. This cosmic information template holds within it the design of the process of expansion and development of the Universe as a coherent unified entity, yet it also facilitates the emergence of all kinds of possibilities as it expands."*[17]

Spangler describes the dynamic of what he calls *"incarnational systems"*:

> *"I find it in the way in which the universal flow of life becomes organised around specific 'attractors' to form patterns, systems, and vortices of energy that are persistent and self-sustaining to some degree. They don't just accumulate energy or substance; they organise it in some persistent manner; they are autopoietic or self-creating. They possess identity and they also have a boundary of some nature that separates them from the rest of the energy flowing around them."* [18]

Wilber [19] notes that people often say that mind creates matter. But he points to a more precise description from the traditional philosophies that would say that *"Mind creates prana; prana creates matter".* In voluntary language, Mind is equivalent to the Container, prana to the Dynamics and matter to the Manifest.

This avoids the tricky question of how matter could have existed billions of years ago when there were no minds. He quotes physicist David Bohm: *"We know of many physical processes, even at the level of quantum phenomena, that do occur without any direct intervention of the observer."* [20] He summarises the argument in this way: *"the perennial philosophy would agree that matter is created out of mind (prana), but through an act of precipitation and crystallisation, not perception and measurement."* [21] Lama Anagarika Govinda describes it through the lens of the mandala in his classic travelogue *The Way of the White Clouds*:

> *"The mandala contains the complete process of the world creation from the deepest centre of consciousness – the unfoldment of forms from the formless state of undifferentiated emptiness (sunyata) and*

unlimited potentiality – through the germ-syllables of the subtle elementary principles and the crystallisation of their essential forms and colours into a concentric image of the Universe, spread out in ever widening rings of materialising worlds."[22]

It even includes the holographic aspect, as *"all the divine figures appear like reflections of the Central and highest truth on different levels of reality."*[23]

Plotinus in his Enneads[24] summarises the Trinity dynamic in his language, where *"Divine Intellect"* is the Container and *"Reason"* or *"Logos"* is the Dynamic.

"The Divine Intellect, then, in its unperturbed serenity has brought the Universe into being by communicating from its own store to matter; and this emanation of the Divine Intellect is Reason (or Logos). This Logos within a seed contains all the parts and qualities concentrated in identity; there is no distinction, no internal hindering; then there comes a pushing into bulk, part rises in distinction from part, and at once the members of the organism stand in each other's way and begin to wear each other down. And while each utters its own voice, all is brought into an ordered system by the ruling Reason."

This completes the thesis for a universal trinity dynamic and a review of different perspectives and traditions that reinforce that thesis.

The next Chapter looks in more details at the Dynamics with its polarity and creative tension arising between the other two aspects of the Trinity, the Container and the Manifest.

[1] *Trinity Binder (1993)*

[2] *Walter Russell - three basic types of words, p8*

[3] *Laszlo (2004)*

[4] *Sheldrake (1981)*

[5] *Nediodow (2014) p87*

[6] *Elgin (1993) p16*

[7] *Radin (2013) xiv*

[8] *Small Wright (1997) p14*

[9] *(personal communication, 7th December 2016)*

[10] *David Spangler (2010) p6*

[11] *David Spangler (2010) p7*

[12] *Bohm (1980)*

[13] *Small Wright (1997) p27*

[14] *Baring, p448*

[15] *Abram (1996) p192*

[16] *Currivan (2005) p41-42*

[17] *Baring (2013) p348*

[18] *Spangler (2010) p72*

[19] *Wilber (1982) p176*

[20] *Wilber (1982) p177-8*

[21] *Wilber (1982) p178*

[22] *Lama Anagarika Govinda (1966) p256*

[23] *Lama Anagarika Govinda (1966) p257*

[24] *quoted in Harvey (1997) p130*

Chapter Two :
Polarity and Potential

The Thesis: *A tension of potentiality (a vacuum or niche) activates the co-creative process from the unified field, leading to fruition and a new integrated life form.*

> *"Surely nature longs for the opposites and effects her harmony from them... That was also said by Heraclitus The Obscure: Combinations – wholes and not wholes, concurring differing, concordant discordant, from all things one and from all one things.*
>
> *"In this way the structure of the Universe – I mean, of the heavens and the Earth and the whole world – was arranged by one harmony through the blending of the most opposite principles."*
>
> **Aristotle, On the World**, *quoted in Harvey*[1]

Volution is the life process that unfolds once an impulse has triggered a movement out of the unified field. As Max Planck said: *"all matter originates and exists only by virtue of a force."*[2]

An impulse is a movement of life that sees an opportunity for a useful experiment arising from an unmet need or unfilled niche, defined by a creative tension between the current reality, including all of the past (the Manifest seed) and a sense of potential in the future (the Container).

This initiating impulse is reflected in the ancient wisdom of the Vedas, where *"desire, aspiration or yearning of the heart is said to have been the first thing, which stirred in the 'deep' at the primordial dawn of all creation."* [3]

The seed is related to raw, instinctual life-creating impulse and embodies the order that enables a coherent whole to emerge:

> *"(Instinct) is a mighty cause which organises the holographic pattern of life forms, the infinite fractal proliferation of itself through countless fields or levels... the source of our creative imagination and our creative power."* [4]

> *"At the first moment of our Universe, literally as space and time began, it was minute and embodied impeccable order. Then rather than in a chaotic explosion, it expanded with amazingly exquisite precision."* [5]

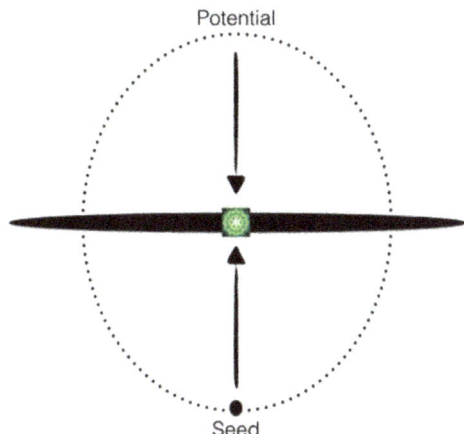

Figure 4 : *The Seed-Potential Polarity*

A tension field is set up between present and future, seed and potential, Manifest and Container, and it is in that polarity that the toroidal dynamics play out. *"It is literally the chicken and egg at the same time."* CG Jung saw polarity being the essence of all life: *"Just as all energy proceeds from opposition, so the psyche too possesses its inner polarity, this being the indisputable prerequisite for its aliveness. Both theoretically and practically, polarity is inherent in all living things."*[6]

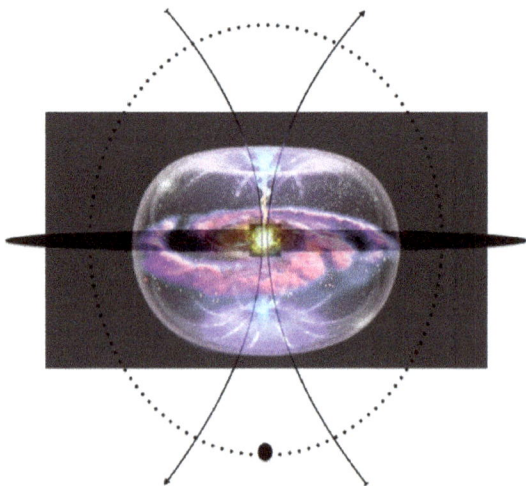

Figure 5 : *A Galactic Torus manifesting from the Polarity*

In the creative tension between the Seed and the Potential, and the gradual interpenetration of the unseen potential with the manifest reality, life starts to take shape and grow – through the heart at the centre.[7] Binder, describing the science of Walter Russell, defines "potential" in a way that fits well with the Potential-Seed polarity described in volution theory: *"Potential is energy wound up ready to*

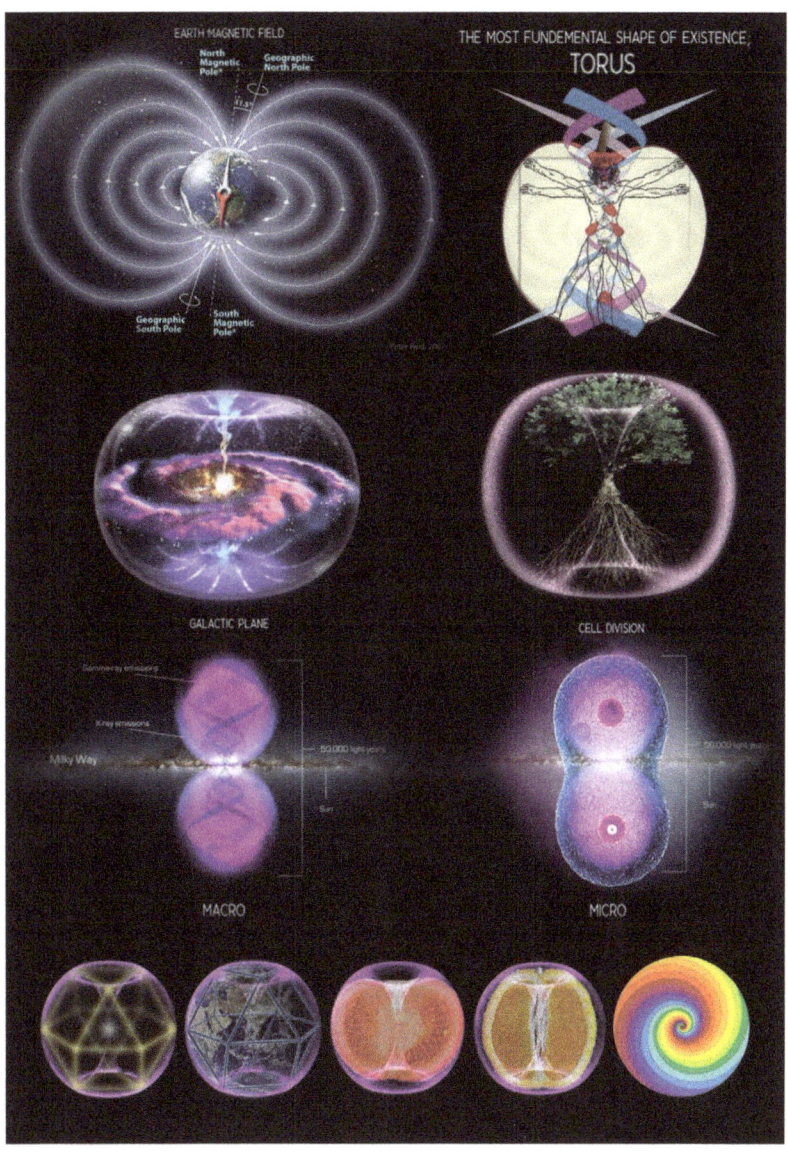

Figure 6 : *Examples of the Torus Form*

Source: Peter Reid, 2007

be released and to penetrate its opposite cone of energy, which is unwound and ready to accept and incorporate its opposite." [8]

This life process can be seen in multiple forms of life, from the smallest to the largest. Figure 6 shows some initial examples of how that actual form shows up in life.

In The Wave, Dr Jude Currivan explains the dynamics of the polarity in a number of different ways. Exploring the meaning of numbers, she notes with the number 2 that *"it is from the interplay of such polarities and their manifold expression, that the world is generated."* [9] Referencing the symbol of the Caduceus (which has been a symbol of healing for millennia), she notes how the two serpents representing the *"interplay and balance of energetic polarities"* are entwined around a third, the staff through which *"they heal into the wholeness of their resolution."* [10]

As mentioned in the previous section, polarity and the number 2 reflect the first dynamic that moves from oneness into relative forms. The vesica pisces (Figure 2) is an oft-used representation of that, with the overlap between the circles representing the space from which 3-dimensional reality is born.

Currivan[11] likewise points to two fundamental binary systems that lie at the core of both our manifest reality and an Eastern understanding of the more hidden dynamics of life. The first is the double-helix structure of DNA, with the bases (A, T, G, C) forming pairs whose *"total number of possible permutations... engenders the 64 so-called DNA codons of the genetic code"*.

The second is the ancient Chinese I Ching, with its matrix of 64 hexagrams that philosopher Martin Schoenberger discovered to have *"exactly the same permutations of binary pairs"* as DNA. From both a scientific and a more esoteric perspective, binary polarities lie at the foundation of all life.

Polarities come back in The Wave[12] in relationship to a vortex field. A torus has a vortex at each end. A vortex field is created by *"eddies of alternative polarities... seen when a stationary object interrupts a moving stream of water or air"*. Plants, Currivan points out, also exhibit this *"alternating rhythm of a three-dimensional vortex sheet as they unfurl around a central stem"*.

Walter Russell was clear in his science that *"matter always forms around gravity poles."*[13] His description of the formation and expansion of form fit well with the volution theory:

> *"Gravity is the centripetally inward-directed motion to compress into form in contrast to radiation as the centrifugally outward-directed motion to expand out of form. In this sense, gravity is the winding up of multicoloured light waves to form ever more dense and more stable matter. Radiation is the unwinding of this same light to form ever more unstable matter."*[14]

In the great wisdom traditions, the idea of the Sacred Marriage of two polar parents making love and giving birth to life is very prevalent. The sacred marriage of sun and moon, god and goddess, king and queen, prince and princess is woven into the rich tapestry of hidden or lost mystical traditions: Alchemy, Gnosticism and the Kabbalah.[15] In the middle of the 20th century, CG Jung stated: *"The assimilation of the fundamental insight that psychic life has two poles still remains a task for the future."* [16]

Govinda describes how critical polarity is to life:

"Flow (of consciousness) means continuity as well as the relationship between two levels or poles. Without this polarity there can be no movement, no life, no awareness – and without continuity no meaningful relationship. The greater the distance of the difference between these two levels or poles, the more powerful is the stream or force that results. The highest consciousness is the product of the widest range of experience: the amplitude between the poles of universality and individuality."[17]

He also illustrates this through a description of Tibetan ritual, with the sublime Buddhas juxtaposed with the *"grotesquely grinning masks"*, seeming to:

"deepen the sense of reality, in which the highest and lowest have their place and condition each other, thus giving perspective and proportion to our conception of the world and of ourselves. By experiencing the opposite pole of realities simultaneously, we actually intensify them. They are like the counterpoints in a musical composition: they widen the amplitude of our emotional response by

creating a kind of inner space through the distance of simultaneously experienced opposites. The wider the amplitude, the greater the depth or intensity of our experience." [18]

Laszlo and Currivan describe the important role of *"duals"* in life, where two aspects of nature mirror each other, *"that are not separate but complementary aspects of each other... such fundamental polarities as the wave/particles of quantum entities and the generic attributes of passive yin active yang principles."* [19]

This creative polarity, with its seed in the moment, the potential in the future and the dynamics of manifestation that follow can also be framed in a different way. In my paper for the Living in Mastery course, I explored the themes of presence, resonance and coherence that had been the focus of the course. I described their relation to the creation process as follows:

"After making explicit the current state of affairs, identifying patterns and releasing the things that hold one there, you then drop into a state of stillness and emptiness (presence), before noticing what is emerging from that empty space and seeing how it starts to take shape (resonance), and then giving it greater form in collaboration with others until it settles into a new pattern (coherence)." [20]

Presence can be seen as the equivalent to the stillness of the seed, resonance as the impulse of the potential from the future, and coherence as what happens as the present and the potential become integrated into a new whole. In the paper, I wrote a poem attempting to express a feeling for those dynamics. [21]

Presence

There is not much

One can say about

Presence

As really it is

Empty

Of anything.

"Empty"

from Old English meaning "rest".

Rest.

Not doing.

Still.

Still.

Not moving.

Noticing movement.

Feeling stillness.

Eye at the centre.

I at the centre.

The centre at I.

I as the centre.

The centre as I.

I as that.

That as I.

I thou it we you its.

Mmmm.

Still.

At rest.

Present

With it all.

Presence.

Something stirs.

Pre-sensing resonance.

Resonance

In the stillness

Something stirs.

Or is stirred.

Still again.

Still. Stir. Still. Stir.

Stir Stir. Still.

Stir Stir Stir. Still.

What's that stirring?

Attention drawn.

Curiosity awakened.

Something is stirring.

The first awake seems to stir others.

New others.

And old others.

New constellation though.

What's stirring?

It's disturbing.

My stillness.

It's growing.

Something is forming.

Strange.

Stranger.

Strangest.

Still is safe.

I know still.

Staying still

I watch the strange stirring.

The connections

Start to draw me in.

I feel excitement.

Something is growing in me.

As me.

It's me growing!

An explosion of stirring

Like the crazed whisking of a spoon in a teacup

Sloshes tea all over the place

Yet is held together by the stirring

At the centre.

Then I see.

The harder is stirred,

The emptier the spiral at the centre

The fuller the tea all around.

Presence holds resonance

As a new form is born.

Bring on the tea!

Coherence

As I see

Myself in the strange

My whole being

Sings a new tune.

From teaspoon

To dervish dancer

Whipping the world into its orbit.

I look up.

Things look different.

They look strange

And I recognise

The strangeness.

It fits.

We fit.

New me, new world.

We move.

We dance.

We sing.

We play.

And stillness fills the movement.

And movement fills the stillness.

As one.

And my mind asks:

But what changed?

I see the same world

But feel it is different.
It responds differently.
I act differently.
But physically it's all the same.
My life is different.
Or so it feels.
What is that out there
If it is so malleable
By this in here?
How can I impact that
When there is so much of it?
What's the difference
Between my experience of reality
And reality itself?
Is there a difference?
What if someone else
Changes their experience of reality
Does that change mine?
And if it's all moving together,
Then who's doing the moving?
That's a conversation killer.
Mind stops.
Still.
In presence
I feel the resonance
And am the coherence
And that's all I know
For now.

A different yet complementary perspective on the role of polarities comes from my experiential study of information and energy and the development of my psychic abilities (meaning competencies that allow me to see more of the subtle spectrum of reality).

For a duration of six classes, I was taught by David McCready to connect more to my psychic intelligence and see different aspects of the subtle energy dimensions more clearly. One exercise involved practicing moving my attention between energetically lighter and heavier/denser dimensions of myself.

I imagined the lighter, more subtle energies as being higher up and the denser, heavier energies being lower down. I noticed that when I rested my attention in the lighter more subtle energies, I experienced lots of light and was unable to distinguish different forms at that level. However, when I brought my attention down to the lower energies and looked up from there at the higher energies, I could clearly distinguish distinct entities in the lighter realms. This is how I recorded it in my journal that day:[22]

> *"Interesting is that it is by sinking in more to the heavier, denser energy that you get to see the lighter energies more distinctly. If trying to see the higher frequencies from the higher frequencies it is just lots of light. As I drop my frequency, I step it down into distincter forms, more refined images."*

This has quite significant implications. Not only does polarity enable the life process to unfold, as argued above, but its very existence allows different aspects on the spectrum of reality to see themselves. From a psychic perspective, I need the denser pole to be able to see and distinguish life forms at the more subtle pole. Only then can I enter into communication with them.

From this perspective, the light pole can be seen as the potential and the dense pole as the seed. It is through the interaction of the poles and the process whereby they enable each other to grow together and integrate, that a person becomes more whole.

This relates to another field of study which underlines polarity's important function in creating new wholeness: the work of Carl Gustav Jung. Anne Baring evokes the importance of polarity in Jung's work:

"Jung's great contribution to an expanded understanding of our nature is that our psychic life has, as it were, two poles. Beyond the conscious mind lies a vast unexplored hinterland – the unconscious." [23]

"Jung defined sickness or neurosis as a state of incompleteness, and health as a state of wholeness brought about through the reconnection of the conscious mind or ego with the unconscious." [24]

"The conscious personality or ego grows and expands through aligning itself with the unseen ground of life. The creation of this relationship over the span of a life is the quintessence of the process of individuation." [25]

Once again, we have a description of a tension field created by two poles, the integration of which leads to a new level of wholeness.

The conscious self, which can be seen as the potential, needs to communicate with and integrate the unconscious mind, which can be seen as the seed. Once this is achieved, the fruit has matured and *"dies"*, becoming a seed for the next iteration.

Currivan[26] describes the thesis of Conformal Cyclic Cosmology developed by Roger Penrose and Vahe Gurzadyan as *"a continuing and holomorphic series of universes, each expanding from big-bang beginnings to an end point that can be reinterpreted as the big bang of the next cycle."* Here the Seed-Fruit dynamic plays out at the cosmological level. Currivan notes the relationship to ancient Vedic notions of creation, described in the Rig Veda as *"innumerable individuated manifestations of consciousness coming into form and then continuing to evolve through countless iterations."* It would appear that scientific and spiritual concepts relate around the idea of the volutionary polar Seed-Fruit process.

In his exploration of time through the works of philosophers Heidegger and Merleau-Ponty; Abram[27] reaches a similar conclusion. He sees the past as having disappeared, *"refusing presence"* and being a foundational support for the present. The future, too, is *"withholding its presence"* and yet both in their own way support the *"perceived landscape"* of the present. As he says, *"sensible phenomena are continually appearing out of, and continually vanishing into, these two very different realms of concealment or invisibility"*. The creative tension between those two poles makes *"possible the open presence of the present"*. He concludes: *"Dare we suspect that these two descriptions describe one and the same phenomenon? I believe that we can, and the isomorphism is complete".* Past and future are two aspects of one volutionary process.

One final point on polarity worth exploring is what happens when the creative potential of a polarity is lost. For a polarity to hold creative tension, both poles must be held in awareness as being equal partners in one system. This allows information to flow into the system to integrate and transcend the poles. If, instead, the poles are seen as opposites that repel and cannot be reconciled, the system is more likely to attract destruction rather than creation.

This is best seen in the realm of conflict. Baring writes: *"Whenever there is a strong polarisation of opposites, there is a situation which attracts shadow projections and the demonising of others."* [28] She quotes Mark Gerzon: *"What marks the Demagogue is that his leadership actually depends on, and is energized by, the existence of a hated Other."* [29]

Destructive entities feed off a repelling polarisation that puts the system into a negative spin, breaking down wholes into parts and regressing to a more divisive consciousness of separation. Creative tension in a polarity leads to a more constructive life-affirming consciousness moving towards greater wholeness and individuation in which each part is increasingly honoured for its specific contribution to the whole.

---

[1]   *Harvey (1997) p117*

[2]   *quoted in Currivan (2017)*

[3]   *Chopra (2007) p23*

[4]   *Baring (2013) p397-398*

5   *Currivan (2017)*

6   *CG Jung (1995) p379*

7   *Merry (2011)*

8   *Binder (1995) p39*

9   *The Wave, Dr Jude Currivan (2005) p32*

10 *The Wave, Dr Jude Currivan (2005) p34*

11 *The Wave, Dr Jude Currivan (2005) p54-55*

12 *The Wave, Dr Jude Currivan (2005) p91*

13 *Binder (1995) p23*

14 *Binder (1995) p23*

15 *Baring (2013)*

16 *CG Jung (1995) p193*

17 *Govinda (1966) p124*

18 *Govinda (1966) p176*

19 *Laszlo and Currivan (2008) p42-43*

20 *Merry (2012) p2*

21 *Merry (2012) p4*

22 *Merry Journal (July 3, 2014)*

23 *Anne Baring (2013) p249*

24 *Anne Baring (2013) p256*

25 *Anne Baring (2013) p260*

26 *Currivan (2017) p193-195*

27 *Abram (1996) p214*

28 *Baring (2013) p314*

29 *Baring (2013) p315*

Chapter Three :
The Holographic Breath

The Thesis: *The volutionary process is a continual flow and exchange between levels of manifestation of varying density (gross/subtle). It is holographic in nature.*

Chapter 2 looked at the polarity arising from an awareness of an unmet possibility and an impulse to fill that niche. The tension between the polarities forms the relational field of potential within which a response to that need can co-creatively emerge.

This chapter focuses on the process that unfolds between those poles in that field of potential: the Dynamics of the Trinity. It covers three main aspects: the surface of the field that is created and held by the polarity (the Container), the geometry of the structure as a whole, and the dynamics playing out inside the entity bounded by the surface, between the poles. I call this the 'holographic breath'.

The Surface Brane

"Some cosmologists believe that what we experience as three dimensional space (and four-dimensional spacetime), may actually be a holographic projection emanating from a two-dimensional boundary termed a brane."[1]

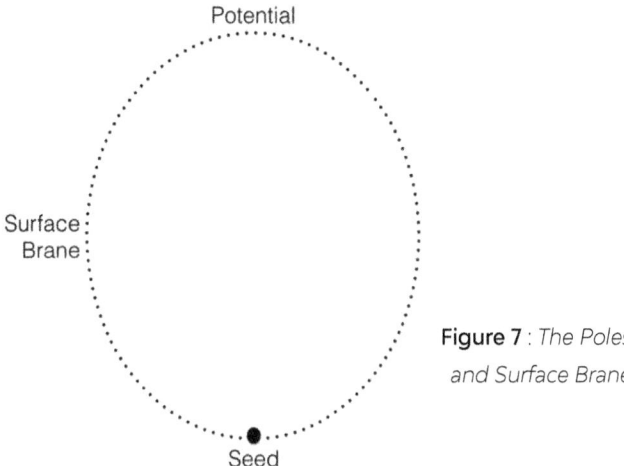

Figure 7 : *The Poles and Surface Brane*

The volution thesis proposes that the process of life is more adequately seen as holographic. This means that information is stored on the surface brane of an entity's Container (created by the initial impulse and polarity).

Nassim Haramein describes it like this from a physics perspective: *"the information that crosses the event horizon of, and is contained within, a black hole is holographically represented on its surface. The event horizon of a black hole has been found to act like a holographic plate, in which all the information within its volume can be represented on its surface area."* [2]

Coherent light from the unified field streams through that surface and literally in-forms the dynamic process of differentiation and interconnection that gives rise to the denser forms of reality that we can perceive.

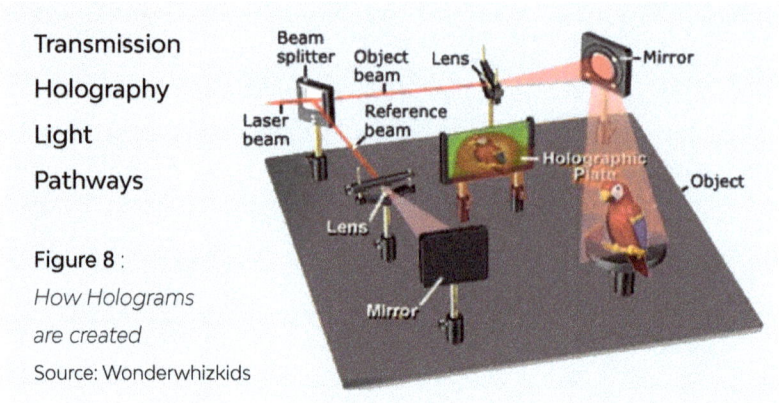

Transmission Holography Light Pathways

Figure 8 :
How Holograms are created
Source: Wonderwhizkids

Figure 8 illustrates the process of imprinting an image onto a holographic plate. A laser beam of coherent, unified light is split into two beams (duality and polarity), one of which passes via the original object (information), while the other is reflected directly onto the holographic plate, where it meets the object beam to create the image.[3]

The above is a more scientific and rational perspective on the process. Another perspective of the same phenomenon, though, can shed light on the inner creative process in people. In his research into how people can impact their reality, Hans Andeweg[4] offers a simple equation: attention plus intention creates a formative force.

A person's intention, Andeweg explains, provides information, whereas attention can be seen as life energy. He describes a co-creative process where someone picks up an idea from a pre-existing information field, then engages that field with their intention and attention, in order to bring it into our physical reality. It is the combination of intention and attention that influences the manifestation process.

If this interior perspective is taken as equivalent to the exterior scientific perspective described above, then the inner intention is equivalent to the object beam that provides the information, and the inner attention is equivalent to the undifferentiated reference beam. The combination of these two serves to imprint the holographic plate and surface brane, thereby providing what is needed for manifestation inside the membrane of the torus. The intention uploads the information, laser-like, for the directionality, while the attention holds open the field of possibilities for that intention to manifest in the form most functional for life.

Talbot quotes scholar Dr George F Dole, who holds degrees from Yale, Oxford, and Harvard, describing Swedenborg's perspective that reflects this dynamic: *"We are constituted by the intersection of two flows – one direct, from the divine, and one indirect, from the divine via our environment. We can view ourselves as interference patterns, because the inflow is a wave phenomenon, and we are where the waves meet."*[5]

The brane surface can be seen as a two-dimensional field. Its function has been described elsewhere by others researching information fields. For example, Rupert Sheldrake describes what he calls 'morphogenetic fields'. These are fields which hold memories from the past relating to collectives (e.g. species of plants and animals, or groupings of people). These fields create patterns which influence probability in the present and future. They *"are responsible for the characteristic form and organisation of systems at all levels of complexity"* and *"affect subsequent similar systems by a cumulative influence that acts across both space and time."*[6]

This can be seen as another description of the brane of the torus. A torus is essentially a rolled up finite surface or brane, that holds information. Talbot describes something similar when he unpacks physicist David Bohm's notion *"that as the present enfolds and becomes part of the past, it does not cease to exist, but simply returns to the cosmic storehouse of the implicate."*[7]

Figure 9 : *The Poles and Surface Brane expressed as a Galaxy*

Currivan[8] references the work of Israeli physicist Jacob Berkenstein, who found that the *"maximum amount of information for a spherical black hole isn't proportional to the three-dimensional volume of space it occupies, but is proportional to its two-dimensional surface area"*, demonstrating that information is related to the two-dimensional brane surface, not the three-dimensional volume.

That information can be seen as being pixelated at the minute Planck scale: *"for each succeeding Planck timescale of 10^{-44} seconds our Universe expresses ever more information, as the past in-forms the present which then in-forms the future."*

The idea of our perceived reality actually being a projection of a more fundamental reality has an earlier expression in Plato's Republic, where he uses the allegory of a dark cave with projections on the back wall of the cave being caused by sunlight streaming in and creating multiple moving shadows. The people in the cave mistake the shadows for reality and forget to look to the source of the shadows as more fundamental. We, too, tend to see the visible world as all there is, whereas a holographic perspective suggests it may be a projection of information stored at a more fundamental level of reality, on the surface of a torus bubble.

In The Wave,[9] Currivan describes the function of membranes as holding information. They are also surfaces that bound an organism. The size of a surface membrane determines how much information a particular organism can hold and handle. For example a *"cell's ability to handle information is proportional to the surface area of the membrane."*[10] The relative amount of information the organism can hold impacts its ability to survive, based on the nature of its dynamic relationship with its environment and its perception of that environment. The more information that is held on the membrane, the more informed the perception of the entity and therefore the more effective it is in engaging with its environment and surviving.

The evolution of multicellular organisms creates a bigger membrane that transcends and includes the cellular membranes. Indeed, the electrical activity in the epidermis - the outer layer of the skin membrane - initiates the regeneration of the physical body. This is where the blueprint information is stored.[11]

The continual expansion of membranes in this way relates to a principle first described by Arthur Koestler and later developed by Ken Wilber: namely holons and holarchies. Wilber states that reality is composed fundamentally of holons, *"wholes that are simultaneously parts of other wholes, with no upward or downward limit."*[12] Holons exist in holarchies, where *"as a more encompassing stage or holon emerges, it includes the capacities and patterns and functions of the previous stage (i.e. of the previous holons), and then adds its own unique (and more encompassing) capacities."*[13]

This matches Currivan's description of the evolution of cell membranes and the brains of vertebrate creatures.[14] The nonlinear emergence of a new holarchical level membrane happens when there are *"a sufficient number of connections between the individual chemical compounds, or nodes, comprising the looping network of catalysis,"*[15] that is, once the current holon membrane has reached a certain stage of integration and coherence.

If, as Wilber suggests, this holarchical pattern that can be seen in membranes and the human brain does in fact describe the nature of all entities in a relative, differentiated world, then we can see how the holographic principle of a surface brane plays out at every new holonic level of a holarchy. As a new level of holon emerges, it transcends yet includes previous levels, expanding its embrace and surface area, and thus its holographic ability to hold more information and deal with greater complexity. This illustrates a key feature of holarchies: they develop in the direction of increasing complexity and differentiation integration[16]. Currivan[17] describes it thus: *"additional, explicit, and transient information is characteristically present just before emergence itself and, crucially, involves an informational dialogue among the pre emergent entity, its subsystems, and its larger milieu."*

In Chapter 4 we will further explore the characteristics of holons and holarchies. For now we continue to focus on the macro-dynamics of volution as expressed through the toroidal form.

The Geometry of the Torus

The torus is one shape that satisfies current cosmological evidence for the design of life. Currivan[18] references scientific research suggesting that our Universe may have a toroidal form. So far we have looked at the role of the surface of the torus, and will look after this section at the flow of the torus. To connect the two we will now look at the geometric structure of the torus.

I was first exposed to the geometry of the torus at the Wisdom University Geometrica intensive in Chartres in 2011. In particular, a moving image of Buckminster Fuller's *"jitterbug"* seemed to pull it all together in what looked very much like a breathing process.

Given that everything emerges out of the unified field, as explored above, what might the geometry of that unified field be? Buckminster Fuller[19] called it the *"Vector Equilibrium"*: *"the zero point for happenings or non-happenings: it is the empty theater and empty circus and empty Universe ready to accommodate any act and any audience."*[20] This equilibrium is ready at any moment to come into movement and create form. This reflects Currivan's first law of information, where information is expressed non-entropically as energy-matter outside of space-time.[21]

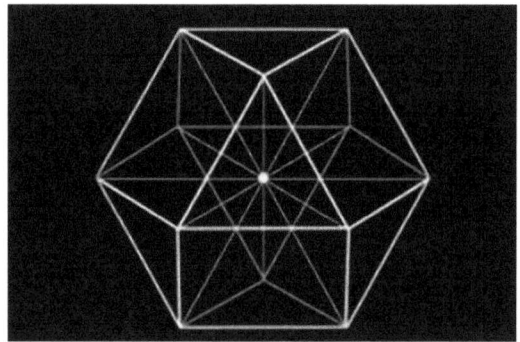

Vector Equilibrium

A Vector Equilibrium is six pairs of vectors, six polarities holding the structure in balance. This is known as *"tensional integrity"*, or *"tensegrity"*,[22] as the tension manifests the form and the form holds the tension. This relates to the concept of the Seed and Potential arising at one and the same moment. It is a moment of conception when a seed planted in the material world is in resonance with its potential in the informational world, forming together an informational envelope within which that life form can crystallise out.

It is literally a process of integration of Heaven and Earth - of in-formation - as potential inspires (*"breathes into"*) physical form and physical form draws down the information through its density and gravity so it can manifest in three-dimensional reality.

This is precisely the process described geometrically by Marshall Lefferts in Cosmometry. Any disequilibrium between the unified field and the Vector Equilibrium releases a dynamic geometry into a process of continual enfolding and unfolding, breathing into the core and out to the periphery, linking up all levels and densities of information, energy and matter.

The density increases as the scale diminishes towards the centre of the entity. As it enfolds and unfolds, the jitterbug passes through the geometric forms of the platonic solids, known to be the core geometries at the foundation of all life forms. The jitterbug dynamic literally links information and energetic potential with material form through its dynamic geometry: it is the creation process.

The concept of seed and flower/fruit to new life can also be seen geometrically through the forms known as the Seed of Life, the Flower of Life and Metatron's Cube.

The six circles of the Seed of Life form the foundation for the expanded Flower of Life, which in turn forms the foundation for the three-dimensional Metatron's Cube that contains within it all the platonic solids, the building blocks of life.[23]

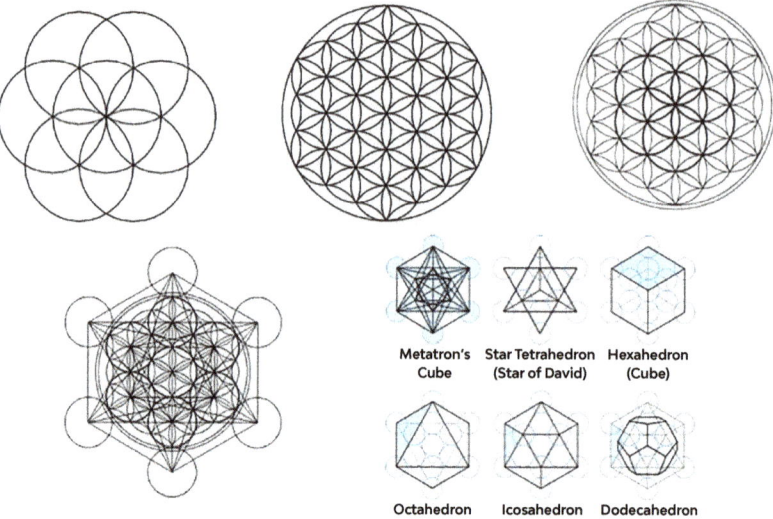

In this process, we see not only the platonic solids, but also the key role played by the phi proportion in the relationships between the parts. Phi, also know as the *"golden proportion"*, is a number that describes the relationship between parts and wholes. It occurs in most natural life forms as the most efficient way of vitalising parts whilst maintaining the coherence of the whole.[24]

As Bateson notes, it enables a spiral to *"retain its shape (i.e., its proportions) as it grows in one dimension by addition at the open end."*[25] This once more demonstrates how the dynamic geometric process seems to reflect natural life dynamics.

Jorn Lehnert[26] calls this geometric form a *"Universo"*: *"The Universo contains all five platonic solids plus two Archimedean solids which are contained within the 64-Tetrahedron-Grid. It is enveloped by the Torus, which surrounds all creation."* His description of the various elements of the geometry is very clear and the colours point to Figure 10:

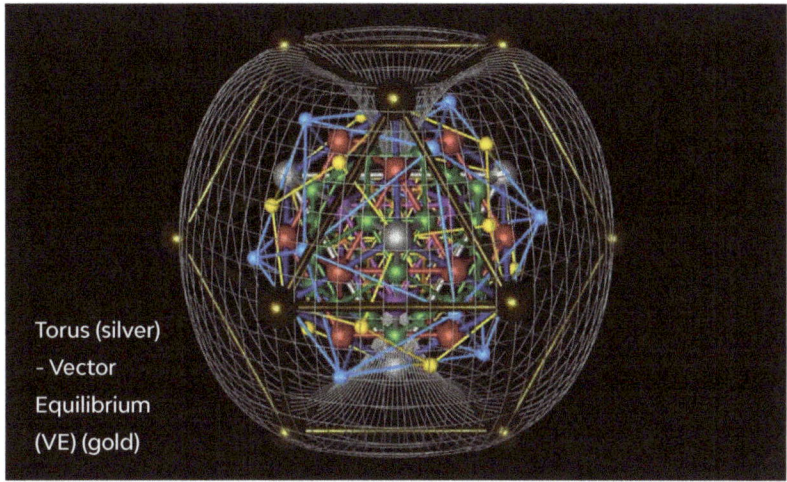

Figure 10 : *Jorn Lehnert's Universo*

1. Out of no-thing - the cubeoctahedron or Vector Equilibrium (VE) (red, orange), an Archimedean solid, emerges with 12 rays from and to the centre. All vectors or rays are equal in length. The VE is a direct expression of singularity. Explosion and implosion are in perfect balance.

2. Two tetrahedrons (platonic solids) (gold, silver), forming the Star-Tetrahedron (Merkaba) inside the hexahedron (cube) (platonic solid) (blue), rotating on its tip.

3. The octahedron (platonic solid) (magenta) touching with its corners the sides of the cube.

4. The rhombicubeoctahedron (green), an Archimedean solid, connecting the VE with the Star-Tetrahedron.

All these solids are contained within and provide the framework for the:

5. 64-Tetrahedron-Grid (Isotropic-Vector-Matrix).

When the tetrahedrons are replaced with spheres and projected on to a 2D surface we get the *"Flower of Life"*.

6. The icosahedron (platonic solid) (sky-blue) and the dodecahedron (platonic solid) (yellow) form an outer shell to complete what is known as *"Metatron's Cube"* in 3D.

7. Torus (silver) and Vector Equilibrium (gold) form the outer shield.

Buckminster Fuller's detailed description of the jitterbug process describes how all these aspects breathe and pulse together, ensuring the continual interaction and distribution of information throughout all levels of the holographic system.[27]

McTaggart[28] describes how this process continually imprints the brane container or *"field"* with all the information from the system, creating what she calls the *"Zero Point Field"* and what Laszlo refers to as the *"Akashic Field."*[29]

Currivan, discussing the mystery schools of Plato and Pythagorus, describes the geometry they discovered as *"the harmonic coherence of fundamental relationships woven into the fabric of space and time,"*[30] seeing the five Platonic solids as *"the universal building blocks of three-dimensional structure and of its interface with spirit."*[31]

Currivan goes on to show how the five aspects of the pentagram bring out the phi relationship described above,[32] connecting the solids in a scalable fractal holographic relationship.[33] This kind of relationship enables the flow of the torus. Currivan summarises how it works:

> *"The informational patterns that underlie our Universe embody the minimum information and simplest instructions at all scales to enable manifestation of the maximum diversity and the development and evolution of the greatest complexity."*[34]

Double Torus

There is compelling evidence that the torus I describe here is not a single torus, but actually a double-twisted torus.[35] The images in Figure 11 show in particular the top view of a magnetic field using ferrofluids where one can see a *"doubly twisted magnetic field,"*[36] which fits with Howard Johnson's discovery of two spinning vortices for magnetic fields.

This relates to physicist Nassim Haramein's double torus thesis.[37] Haramein illustrates how the double torus dynamic can be seen in the way galaxies and black holes work. His description of how a particle flows through a double torus (Figure 12), shows it coming out at ninety degrees from the space where it is most contracted at the centre,

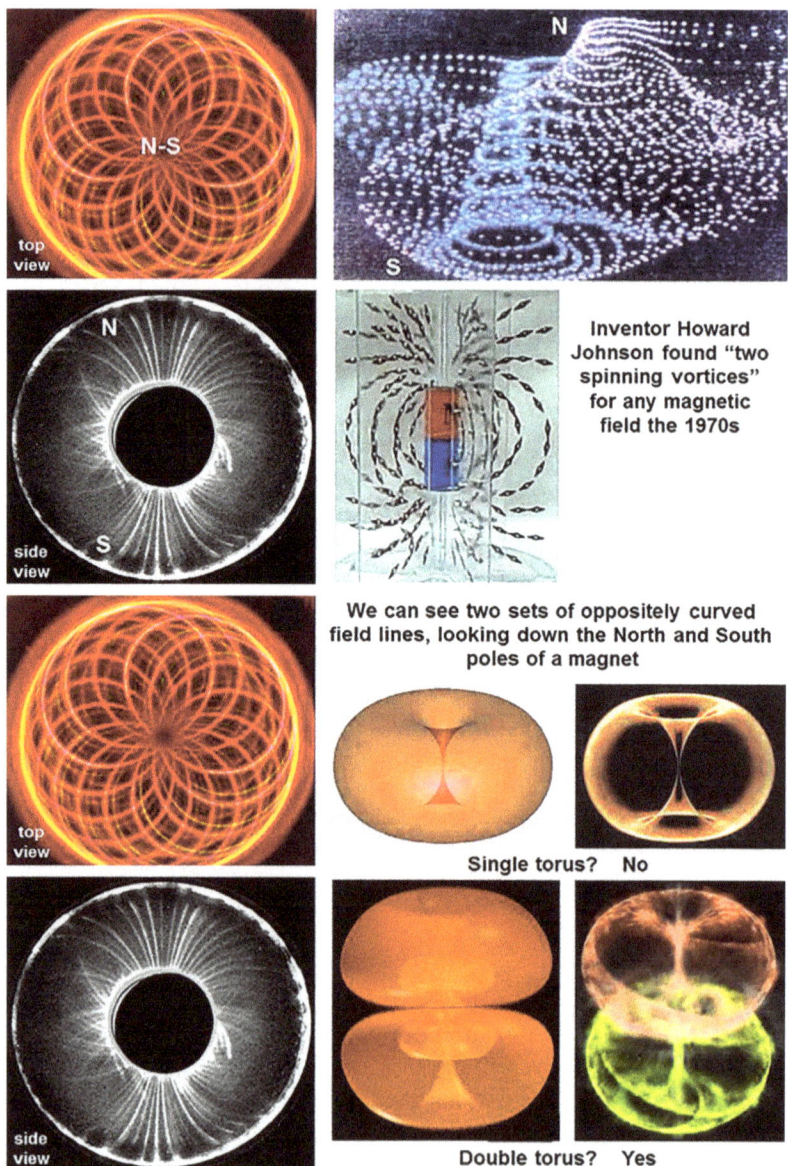

Figure 11 : *Anasazi on Magnetic Fields and the Double Torus*

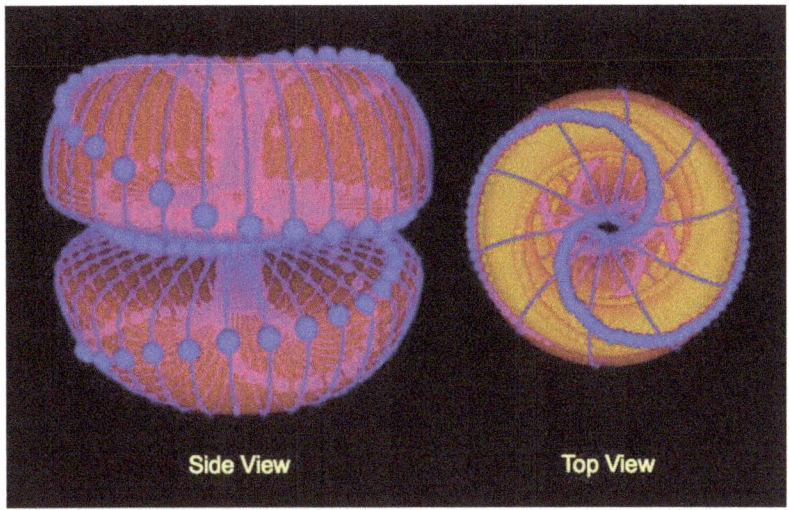

Figure 12 : *Haramein's Double Torus*   Animations courtesy of Robert Gray

backing up the thesis that the material world manifests at a ninety degree plane to the non-material *"The underlying informational field is embedded and embodied in so-called phase space... The complex plane of phase space is geometrically 90° out of phase with the materialised world."*[38]

For Haramein, this explains how the Universe is seen to both expand and contract in parallel. The expansion is perceived on the outer surface of the torus, and the contraction happens at the centre. There is both a movement towards differentiation in the expansion and towards interrelatedness in the contraction. I can see it as the potential-seed torus reflected as in a mirror. In the double torus the information flows in from the top of the upper torus and the bottom of the lower torus. The seeds are therefore both in the middle which is what gives rise to the manifestation of the relative reality. The two seeds could be seen as the original yin-yang or fire-ice before they differentiate.

Elgin describes two attributes of a torus that also support the expansion and contraction dynamic. A torus is both *"dynamically closed (as self-organising and self-bounding systems) and dynamically open (directly connecting with the Meta-Universe)."*[39] The self-referencing nature of the closure supports contraction while the open connection enables continual expansion.

Haramein also notes how, in esoteric traditions, the top and bottom chakras are portrayed as vortices bringing in energy from above and below and meeting at the heart - with the heart chakra depicted as the star of David, or star tetrahedron (Figure 13). Andeweg's ECOintention practice, too, depicts the integration of the conceptual and manifest energies in this way (Figure 14).

Figure 13 : *Depiction of the Heart Chakra*

Andeweg[40] relates this integration process to Metatron's cube as above, together with the Huna vision of a person and the Flower of Life.

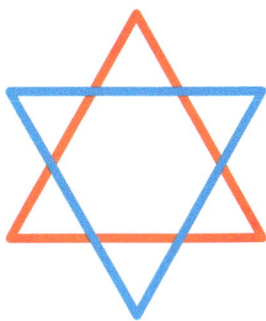

Figure 14 : *Andeweg'sIntegration of Concept (blue) and Realisation (red)*

In his depiction (Figure 14), Andeweg also identifies the creative polarity between the Higher self of potential (what he also calls the *"gate of appearance,"* as that is where the information appears in its quest to become form) and the seed of Deeper self, with the manifestation process happening in the space in between. His nine levels align with the volutionary octave as he has the central level as the heart, where in volution the heart sits between the two central phases of the octave.

Another point of interest is how, when seen from above, the double torus reflects the Seed of Life symbol, containing the geometry of the platonic solids and proportions of life.[41]

Anastazi notes another important feature: even though there is a vortex at each of the two poles, there is still a net flow of energy in one direction. From a volutionary perspective that could imply that the pole of Potential holds a greater pull than the Seed pole, reflecting the general directionality of increasing unity and differentiation, moving into an integration that transcends yet includes the parts. If the poles held each other in equal balance, there would be no dynamic or direction.

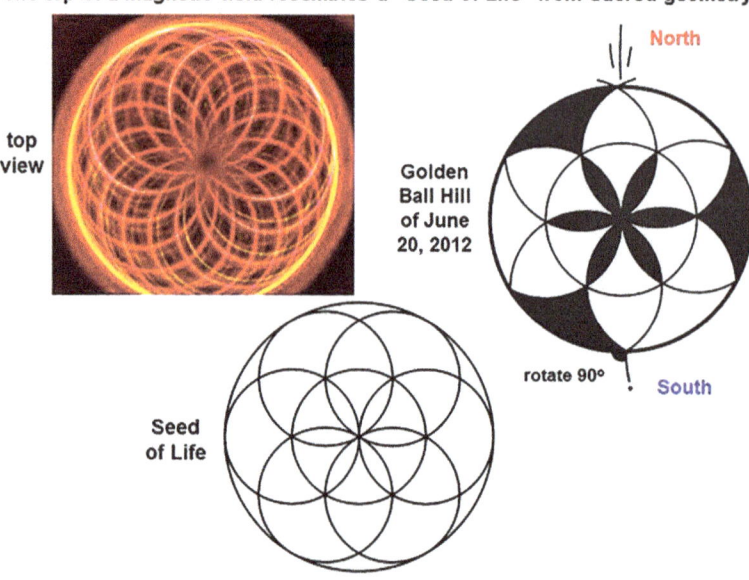

Figure 15 : *Magnetic fields and the Seed of Life*   (Anastazi 2012)

The Flow of the Torus

"Every action starts from an intention in the implicate order. The imagination is already the creation of the form; it already has the intention and the germs of all the movements needed to carry it out. And it affects the body and so on, so that as creation takes place in that way from the subtle levels of the implicate order, it goes through them until it manifests in the explicate."[42]

The idea of the life process being a breathing pulsating process goes back a long way. In ancient India's Vedic tradition, the Universe was seen as the cyclic breath of Brahman. From these age-old perspectives through to modern scientific understanding, the torus is seen as a fundamental element of life. Modern research in biology is discerning toroidal and fractal dynamics. Meijer and Geesink[43] state in their summary:

> *"In our brain a toroidal integration of phonon, photon and electron fluxes may guide information messengers such as Ca2+ ions to induce coherent oscillations in cellular macromolecules. The integration of such multiple informational processes is proposed to be organised in a fractal 4-D toroidal geometry, that is proposed to be instrumental in conscious perception."*

In The Wave, Currivan refers to water researcher Viktor Schauberger:

> *"From his deep knowledge of water, Schauberger was able to extend the principles of its energy flow to a generic realisation that nature consistently uses vortical spiralling motion which is implosive or centripetal for creating and evolving – and conversely the explosive or centrifugal form of motion for dissolution and decomposition."*[44]

Referring to the centripetal and centrifugal forces, Schauberger points to an important aspect of volution and the toroidal form that we looked at above: polarity. In relation to Chapter 2 on the polarity of the potential and seed in volution, we can recognise the centripetal generative force as the incoming formative force from the potential pole, and the centrifugal force as the outgoing expressive force of the seed pole.

The centripetal generative force of the potential shapes the material form present in the seed; the expressive centrifugal force of the seed manifests that potential outwards. The Aizawa Attractor in mathematics is a great visual reflection of this toroidal process (see link in the notes). It seems to create structure from the chaos, giving us a sense that we are surrounded by unseen forces beyond our comprehension." [45]

The esoteric tradition of theosophy makes a similar connection between these forces and the torus:

> *"The toroidal form is caused by some initiating energy meeting resistance from another force that causes it to curl back upon itself into concentric circular sheaths or waves... The two great forces of centripetal and centrifugal motion create the tension that gives form to the formless."* [46]

This toroidal dynamic of creative tension between the poles continues until *"either the original impulse has been neutralised by the secondary energy (inertia) or the primary force is sufficiently strong enough to impose a new and greater rhythm on a lesser force or energy."*

This would suggest that the life form and its torus continue to exist and evolve either until the seed has done all it can to express the potential or the potential has transformed the seed into something able to express more of life that it was originally designed for. It also suggests that life force is maintained through an ongoing relationship and creative tension between potential stored in informational fields (the Container) and physical reality (the Manifest).

Currivan[47] notes the work of neurophysiologist Ralph Gerard who *"has found that nerves throughout the human body are uniformly polarised; positive at the inputs fibre (or dendrite) and negative at the outputs fibre (or axon), guiding electrical impulses to move in one direction only and thus giving electromagnetic coherence to the nervous system."* Once more, we encounter a natural system whose vitality and functioning is maintained by a polarity with input one end and output the other end.

In my research into crop circles, I discovered a process that also looked remarkably like volution at work.[48] I concluded that the formations emerge out of the interaction between a vertical electromagnetic axis and a horizontal sound axis. Sound carries the information of the pattern and flattens the crop in an electromagnetic tension field between in a polarity sky and earth.

Hardy, in her exploration of nonlocal resonance between people, describes what she sees psychically in the field of activity. She calls these fields *"Telhar fields (telepathic-harmonic fields)"*[49] and creates an image of it that looks just like a torus with a ninety degree plane.

The nature of spin relates to the creative relationship between the centripetal potential force and the centrifugal seed force. There is a

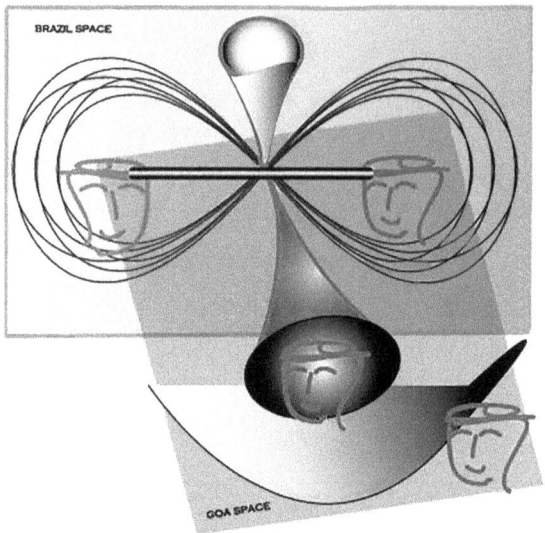

Figure 16 : *Chris Hardy's depiction of the "Telhar Field" during her Nonlocal Experience of a Dance Event in Goa*

dynamic in the physical sciences called the *"conservation of angular momentum"* whereby, as the periphery approaches the axis, like a skater pulling in their arms, the spin accelerates, and vice-versa. The centripetal potential force brings the periphery in towards the centre, giving the entity density, shape and coherent form. The centrifugal force pushes out from centre, expressing itself in increasing uniqueness. A healthy life form has a good balance between the two. If it is too internally directed centripetally, then it doesn't express its potential in the world. If it is too dispersed in its centrifugal expression, then it loses touch.

Walter Russell, whose diagrams and art work are outlined in Binder, described reality in a very similar way. Here are two of his diagrams:

Relationship of the Still White Light to Form

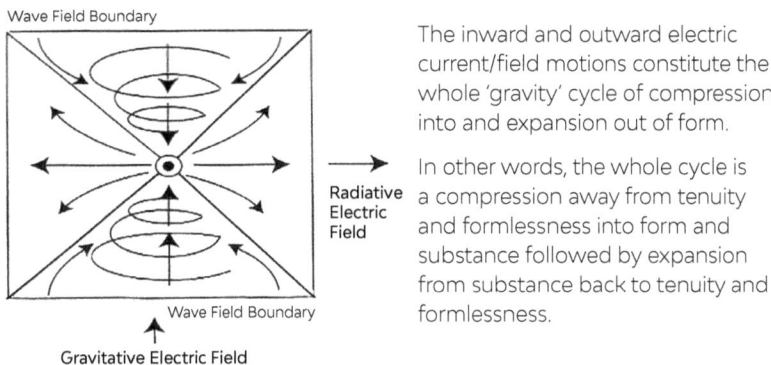

The inward and outward electric current/field motions constitute the whole 'gravity' cycle of compression into and expansion out of form.

In other words, the whole cycle is a compression away from tenuity and formlessness into form and substance followed by expansion from substance back to tenuity and formlessness.

Figure 17 : *Walter Russell on Electric Field Motions*

'Gravitation' Flow

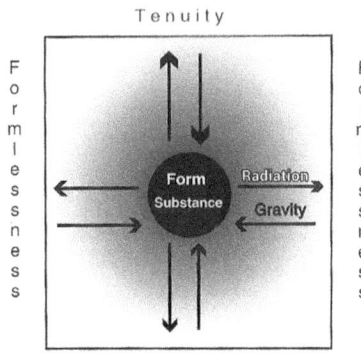

The simulation of the still white 'magnetic' light occurs at the spherical center of the wave/ field/system. The wave axis, the cube wave boundary, and the inner reflecting radar planes are the dividing/connecting lines of relationship that represent the still white 'magnetic' light in the relative Universe.

The One undivided light of the mind at rest is the still magnetic white light which is everywhere at once in the whole Universe and which cannot be sensed anywhere in the relative sensed universe.

Figure 18 : *Walter Russell on Radiation and Gravity*

Figure 17 shows the toroidal dynamic with the compression and expression of form at the centre: *"a compression away from tenuity and formlessness into form and substance followed by expansion from substance back to tenuity and formlessness."*[50] Figure 18 illustrates the same phenomena together with the parallel processes of compression (*"Gravity"*) and expansion (*"Radiation"*).

This dynamic balance between the centripetal and centrifugal enables the flow of information through the system. Currivan, Jahn & Dunne and Roney-Dougal[51] all document research on *"presentiment"*, that is, the experience of knowing something before it seems to manifest in our three-dimensional visible world. Radin[52] documents research showing how *"the present is also influenced by the future"*. Currivan suggests that, rather than thinking of this phenomenon as somebody sensing the future (which is what it looks like if you take a linear time perspective on it), it is more adequate to see it as the person accessing the information that already exists in the information fields a relatively short time before it shows up in the gross physical realm.[53]

Bohm reinforces this: *"When people dream of accidents correctly and do not take the plane or ship, it is not the actual future that they were seeing. It was merely something in the present which is intricate and moving toward making that future"*.[54] Abram backs up this perspective with his research into how Heidegger and Merleau-Ponty describe time. Heidegger, he says, *"writes of the past and present as absences that by their very absence concern us, and so make themselves felt within the present."*

He describes Merleau-Ponty's position on our need to locate things in a past or future as *"searching for certain invisible aspects of the visible environment, certain unseen regions whose very hiddenness somehow enables or makes possible the open visibility of the land around us."*[55] For both these philosophers, the past and future do not exist outside of the present but are aspects of it.

This is an example of how the flow of information works in a toroidal system. Before information crystallises into denser form it exists in a less dense form and can be accessed by extending the ability of our awareness to be able to pick up information in more subtle stages. Our brain already does that unconsciously as Radin[56] has demonstrated. Currivan[57] references an experiment by a team of physicists at the University of Geneva who demonstrated how the information present in a photon was actually preserved after the physical destruction of the photon itself, suggesting that information is connected to but not limited by the physical form it takes.

She also references Michael Levin and colleagues at Tufts University who *"have shown that Planaria flatworms aren't just able to regenerate their heads, but when they do so they remember information they knew before decapitation."*[58] The information supersedes the form (which also reinforces the case made in Chapter 1 for seeing the Soul as the information-holding brane field of an entity - the information exists outside of the time-space manifestation of the form).

This holographic breath flows between more dynamic potential and denser manifestation. The relative density of reality relates to the coherence of wave forms. Information expresses itself as energy-matter. As Currivan points out, *"Physics has now equated matter with energy. The perceived separation of material objects has been replaced by energy fields, which incorporate harmonic patterns and waves."*[59]

Matter forms through coherent waves of energy. This positive interference of waves enables the holographic process described above.[60] Information streams through the torus-like entity expressing itself as energy in relatively dense or subtle forms, creating the holographic reality that all information is always present in each of the parts of the system. This last point is backed by research into memory, which has been shown to exist throughout the brain like a hologram, not just in one part of the brain.[61]

In the holographic volution concept, how the roles of information and energy are defined is important. A good example is how healing works. Currivan notes that *"it is not energy that heals, but the information, and perception it carries. Thoughts and emotions are patterns of energy configuration and it is the rearrangement of these patterns, which either inhibit or restore health."*[62]

Stanislav Grof's important work on the healing of the individual and collective points once more to the holographic and fractal nature of life. Grof illustrates connections between the perinatal phases of development (four basic perinatal matrices, BPMs I-IV) and societal themes.[63] People experience different images of the world depending on the BPM they are accessing during a healing process. This can be summarised as follows:

BPM 1   (intra-uterine existence) - ideal social structure, ideal world.

BPM 2   (first phase of birth - contractions) - oppressive and abusive totalitarian societies; focus on larger system.

BPM 3 (second phase of birth - continued contractions and into birth canal) - bloodiness and goriness; focus on more detailed, intimate experience of violence.

BPM 4 (actual moment of birth and separation from mother) - victory in wars, liberation, celebration.

This points to the possibility that the individual's inner experience in these perinatal phases resonates at an archetypal level with experiences in our collective human field, and vice-versa. If indeed reality is fractal in this way, then as we transform our traumas at the individual level we could also be changing the patterns in the collective field.

Grof asserts that without the inner transformation of the traumas we will not solve the equivalent problems in the world. Likewise, were we collectively to face up to the pain we cause each other and other life on this planet, as in the despair and empowerment work of Joanna Macy,[64] then we would be helping individuals to clear any trauma they had experienced in the perinatal phases.

Next we look at how holographic patterns show up in this flow process. David Bohm coined the word holomovement[65] to describe both the holographic nature of the Universe and its toroidal flow.

Holographic Patterns

This volutionary structure, dynamic and flow gives rise to the holographic presence of similar patterns across all expressions of life. Wilber describes it in this way:

"According to the perennial philosophy, not only does this whole process of involution play itself out over centuries, it repeats itself moment to moment, ceaselessly and instantaneously."[66]

Currivan lists many of those patterns occurring in the frequency and intensity of phenomena such as conflicts, earthquakes, language, urban development and more general human activity. Researchers have found that the Internet reflects patterns in ecosystems: *"the expansion of the Net has revealed emergent properties that can be modelled using precisely the same mathematical tools as those to study biological ecosystems."*[67] This further reinforces the perspective that human expression and creativity are one more expression of life, in the same way that ecosystems are. Ultimately we are the Earth expressing itself through the same universal patterns as all life. As Currivan concludes:

"as more and more analyses of human activities are investigated, it's becoming increasingly clear that while arising from myriad individual decisions, our group and collective conducts embody exactly the same holographic signatures as are exhibited throughout the so-called "natural" world."[68]

Recent scientific studies also point towards a holographic design of the Universe. A study by the University of Southampton,[69] in association with three other universities, *"has provided what researchers believe is the first observational evidence that our Universe could be a vast and complex hologram."*

To summarise this chapter: I have been looking at the dynamics of the flow between the two poles of seed and potential that create the container for something to express itself in life. I have proposed that those dynamics are holographic and toroidal in nature, that the container field resembles a membrane that holds information and expands, that there is a geometry to the torus and that the toroidal dynamic is like a breath with a continual flow between denser and more subtle energetic expressions of information. The holographic nature of the Universe leads to similar patterns showing up across all expressions of life.

In the following chapter I will look at how the poles grow towards each other, the subtle interpenetrating the gross and vice-versa, and how this is a process whereby an entity becomes increasingly whole and conscious of itself, until it reaches full fruition.

---

[1] *Currivan (2005) p69*

[2] *https://www.resonancescience.org/*

[3] *Talbot (1991) p15*

[4] *(2011) p95*

[5] *(1991) p259*

[6] *Rupert Sheldrake (1981) p3*

[7] *Talbot (1991) p200*

[8] *Currivan (2017) p35-36*

[9] *Currivan, The Wave, p164-166*

[10] *Currivan, The Wave, p164*

[11] *Currivan, The Wave, p216*

[12] *Ken Wilber (1995) p35*

[13] *Ken Wilber (1995) p20*

[14] *Currivan, The Wave, p166*

15 *Currivan, The Wave, p168*

16 *Wilber (1995) p67-68*

17 *Currivan (2017)*

18 *Currivan (2017) p102-104*

19 *Buckminster Fuller (Edmondson 2009)*

20 *Fuller (1975)*

21 *Currivan (2017)*

22 *Edmondson, A, (2009)*

23 *Melchizedek (1990)*

24 *Doczi (2005)*

25 *Bateson (1979) p12*

26 *Jorn Lehnert (2014)*

27 *Edmondson (2009) p179-193.*

28 *McTaggart (2001) p26*

29 *Laszlo (2004)*

30 *Currivan (2005) p29*

31 *Currivan (2005) p39*

32 *Currivan (2005) p43*

33 *Currivan (2005) p46*

34 *Currivan (2017)*

35 *Haramein (2011), Anasazi (2012)*

36 *Anasazi (2012)*

37 *Haramein (2011)*

38 *Laszlo & Currivan (2008) p57*

39 *Elgin (1993) p209*

40 *Andeweg (2016)*

41 *Anastazi (2012)*

42 *David Bohm in Talbot (1991) p84*

43 *Meijer and Geesink (2016)*

44 *Currivan, The Wave (2005) p181*

45 *https://dynamicmath.xyz/calculus/velfields/Sprott/*

[46] *Carpenter & Sarelas (2010)*

[47] *Currivan (2005) p215*

[48] *https://petermerry.org/crop-circles-how-they-appear-and-what-they-show-us/*

[49] *Hardy (2008) p2*

[50] *Binder (1995) p21*

[51] *Currivan (2005), Jahn & Dunne (2005) and Roney-Dougal (2010)*

[52] *Radin (2013) p108, 133-178*

[53] *Currivan (2005) p142-145*

[54] *Bohm, quoted in Talbot (1991) p212*

[55] *Abram (1996) p212*

[56] *Radin (2004)*

[57] *Currivan (2017) p52*

[58] *Currivan (2017) p156*

[59] *Currivan (2005) p89*

[60] *Currivan (2005) p94*

[61] *Currivan (2005) p119*

[62] *Currivan (2005) p220*

[63] *Stanislav Grof (2012) p166-167*

[64] *Macy (1998)*

[65] *David Bohm (1980)*

[66] *Wilber (1982) p163*

[67] *Currivan (2017) p166*

[68] *Currivan (2017) p178*

[69] *University of Southampton (2017)*

Chapter Four :
An Octave Perspective

The Thesis: *The journey from seed impulse to mature fruition can be described as an octave of 8 phases. The mature form (fruit) becomes the seed for the next level of the process, if there is a niche for it to respond to. It may also have fulfilled its function and just dissolve.*

The Octave

This section goes into more detail about the phases of growth within a holographic torus-like entity as it moves from seed to fruit. I have chosen to explore this through the lens of eight phases, as an octave, for a number of reasons.

Firstly, I initially came to my insights on volution through the exploration of the eight levels of Spiral Dynamics in a rigorous body-based workshop process, which I shall describe below. Secondly, the octave has always been known as a complete set, with the eighth note bringing completion to a scale. This fits the idea of seed growing into fruit, the octave both completing one scale of notes and starting another. Lastly, as I read more, I came across a number of other points reinforcing the validity of this exploration. We shall consider these first, before moving on to the details. I do want to note that the octave perspective is only one possible perspective on the volution dynamics of a living entity; other perspectives, too, would surely yield interesting insights. What is key in the octave perspective is the doubling of frequency, whether you take a scale of eight notes or a chromatic scale of 12 or 13. As we shall see in a later section, we can also build on our insights into the Spiral Dynamics model's eight stages to link volution to human individual and cultural development.

In The Wave, Currivan makes several references to the octave and the significance of the number 8. From a sound perspective, she notes that the eighth note in an octave *"represents a sound whose wavelength is exactly half and thus whose frequency is twice the first note. This 2 to 1 ratio of wavelength and frequency is repeated with each higher octave and represents a fundamental property of energetic waves, called resonance."*[1] The seed (1) and potential (8) come into resonance with each other, healing ("whol-ing') and sealing the entity. From a numerological perspective, she notes that *"the essence of the number eight is the continual weaving together of the world of energy."*[2]

From the scientific perspective of chemistry, she points out that rows in the periodic table *"complete the expression of the properties in an eight-step cycle or octave, which was eventually discovered to relate to the completion of orbital shells of electrons at different energetic states around the atomic nuclei."*[3] From a geological perspective, she notes that *"The Gutenberg-Richter power law of earthquakes shows that when their magnitude doubles, their frequency is reduced by a factor of four – this 2:1 relationship represents the harmonic of the octave."* [4]

From an esoteric perspective, she discusses the need and evidence for an eighth chakra to complete the traditional seven, and notes that *"Only when we resonate to a higher octave of awareness do we begin to fully comprehend the wholeness of who we really are."* [5]

Elgin also references an *"eighth dimension"* in which *"the polarities of life will be integrated continuously into a higher synthesis."* [6] He believes that at that eighth stage in human development we will come to see *"the entire Universe as continuously woven together as a single, flowing creation"*, and *"a holographic entity, where all is contained within all"* [7] and that the torus is the most adequate geometric form to represent that. [8]

Timothy Leary [9] defines an eight circuit model of consciousness that has also been mapped onto other models of eight as in the tables opposite. Note the significance of the half-way point that is also key in the volution process.

This shows that it is possible to make a good case for describing a complete entity using the number eight and the octave.

Dylan Newcomb [10] notes how the octave is also an expression of three polarity dimensions, making possible a link between the trinity described above and the octave.

Timothy Leary's Eight-Circuit Brain Model in the New Hermetics *1*				
BIO-CIRCUIT	**EVOLUTIONARY PROCESS**	**ACTIVATION IN HUMAN GROWTH**	**AREA OF CONSCIOUSNESS**	**DRIVING FORCES**
I **Biosurvival**	one-celled life	infant	sucking, nourishment, cuddling	pain/pleasure
II **Emotional-Territorial**	vertebrate life	toddler	power struggles	dominance/ submission
III **Semantic**	early primate, language and tools	child	learning, calculation	intelligence/ stupidity
IV **Socio-Sexual**	urbanized civilization	post-pubescent domesticity	morality, reproduction, pair-bonding	right/ wrong
V **Neurosomatic**	neurological and somatic consciousness explorers	ecstatic consciousness	bliss, somatic rapture	euphoria
VI **Neuroelectric**	advanced consciousness engineers	metaprogramming consciousness	reprogramming self, relativization of reality	creativity
VII **Neurogenetic**	superior consciousness engineers	evolutionary consciousness	collective unconscious	evolution
VIII **Neuroatomic**	superlative consciousness engineers	quantum consciousness	non-local awareness, cosmic union	omnipresence

Table 2 : *Timothy Leary's Eight-Circuit Brain Model In the New Hermetics 1*

Retrieved from **newhermetics.com**

Timothy Leary's Eight-Circuit Brain Model in the New Hermetics *2*			
BIO-CIRCUIT	**QABALISTIC SEPHIRA**	**NEW HERMETICS LEVEL**	**POWER**
I **Biosurvival**	10. Malkuth	Initiate	control of pain and pleasure
II **Emotional-Territorial**	9. Yesod	Zealot	control of emotions
III **Semantic**	8. Hod	Practitioner	control of beliefs
IV **Socio-Sexual**	7. Netzach	Philosopher	control of values
V **Neurosomatic**	6. Tiphareth	Adept	communion with cosmic consciousness
VI **Neuroelectric**	5. Geburah	Advanced Adept	creativity within cosmic consciousness
VII **Neurogenetic**	4. Chesed	Perfect Adept	integration within cosmic consciousness
VIII **Neuroatomic**	3. Binah	Master	identification with cosmic consciousness

Table 3 : *Timothy Leary's Eight-Circuit Brain Model In the New Hermetics 2*

Retrieved from **newhermetics.com**

In his work with the I Ching, he describes how one polarity dimension is simply Yin and Yang, or Other and Self. As that dimension differentiates to a second dimension, we get Yin-Yang-Yin-Yang, and the core dynamic of differentiation (Yin) and integration (Yang). One more differentiation goes to three dimensions and an octave of 4 Yins and 4 Yangs, with a core dynamic of contract (Yin) and expand (Yang).

The first dimension, which he relates to the first person Subject, can be seen as the volutionary seed of the present moment. The third dimension, which he relates to the third person Object, can be seen as the Potential out there that is seen in the future. The second dimension, which he relates to the Verb, being the relationship between Subject and Object, can be seen as the process of differentiation and integration. In this way the trinity and the octave are integrated.

Newcomb 3D and Octave										Volution
Newcomb		i Ching								**Volution**
3D Object	−	+	−	+	−	+	−	+		Potential
2D Verb	−		+		−		+			Integration Process
1D Subject	−				+					Seed

Table 4 : *Newcomb 3D and Octave*

Eight Phases

It is now time to turn to the detail of the eight phases. As mentioned above, this draws on the Spiral Dynamics model,[11] a theory of human individual and collective development that evolved from the work of Dr Clare W Graves.[12] The model essentially describes the evolution of underlying values systems in people and societies from survival onwards. The idea that humanity has evolved through a linear process over time is probably one of the most widely accepted ideas across the human species.

There is debate between more religious fundamentalist perspectives and more scientific-rational perspectives about exactly when it all began (e.g. a few thousand years ago versus 14 billion years ago), but they all agree on the idea that since that beginning we have been evolving through historical time with a past, present and future.

Indeed, even our most popular philosophers and spiritual teachers tend to promote an evolutionary perspective.[13] In my own book [14] I adopted and connected these various evolutionary theories.

However, over recent years I have come to question this perspective, and the volution theory emerged from that inquiry. The map of the territory of our human development that I am most familiar with is Spiral Dynamics,[15] together with Wilber's archetypal dynamics of that journey.[16] Based on the research of Clare W Graves,[17] it describes the evolution of our individual and collective worldviews, oscillating between I-centred and We-centred perspectives, in interaction with the life conditions as we experience them around us.

Here is a summary of the worldviews:

LEVEL 1st Tier	GRAVES CODE	I -SELF	WE -CULTURE	ITS -STRUCTURES
Beige	Express self for physiological survival	Instinctual Self	Archaic	Survival Clans
Purple	Sacrifice self to maintain the ways of old	Magic Self	Animistic -magical	Ethnic Tribes
Red	Express self impulsively at any cost without shame or fear	Ego-centric Self	Power Gods	Feudal Empires
Blue	Sacrifice self for reward later	Mythic Self	Mythic Order	Nation States
Orange	Express self for self-gain, but calculatedly	Achiever Self	Scientific Rational	Corporate States
Green	Sacrifice self to get acceptance now	Sensitive Self	Pluralistic	Value Communities
2nd Tier				
Yellow	Express self with concern for, and not at the expense of, others	Integral Self	Integral	Integral Commons
Turquoise	Sacrifice self to existential reality	Holistic Self	Holonic	Holistic

Figure 19 : *Spiral Dynamics Eight Stages* Merry 2009

Graves, and Beck and Cowan after him, postulate that our evolution is a never-ending quest, with one world view's solutions sowing the seeds for the next set of existential problems, which a new world view then emerges to solve.

During the very first course I followed with Dr Don Beck on Spiral Dynamics, I remember saying to him that it seemed to me that the model Spiral Dynamics came out of a Yellow Integral world view, and that therefore once we get to Holistic Turquoise, we should expect the model itself to start to look out-dated and a more adequate model to emerge. He replied: *"I like the way you think, Peter Merry"*. That was the start of a great relationship.

Now it feels like the Turquoise moment has come, and in the very spirit of what lies at the heart of Spiral Dynamics, it is time to expand our current understanding while embracing the best of what it has given us so far.

From Worldviews to Energy Dynamics

In my work with Dylan Newcomb, exploring the energy dynamics of the Spiral Dynamics value systems through the body, we settled on a framing that held to the set of eight worldviews.

One reason for this was that we didn't feel we could stretch much beyond Turquoise ourselves, and that there was very little data on Turquoise itself, let alone anything postulated to exist beyond it. Other reasons for working with the eight were Newcomb's musical background and the natural form of an octave, and my sense that the model would shift anyway when we got beyond Yellow. It is important to remember that this was a choice, that therefore gave us data from that octave perspective.

When we started to explore the spiral through the octave lens, some interesting insights emerged that formed the beginning of my inquiry into a new framing. One of the key findings was a relationship between

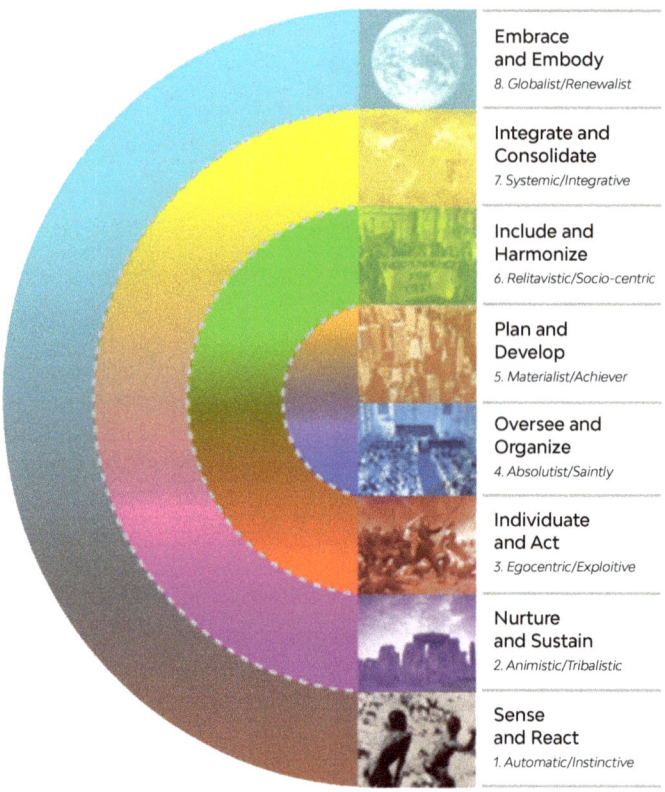

Figure 20 : *Spiral Dynamics Stages Relationships*
Newcomb D, personal communication, 2011

Beige (1) and Turquoise (8), Purple (2) and Yellow (7), Red (3) and Green (6), Blue (4) and Orange (5), as depicted in Figure 20.

The body-based research that we carried out around this involved having dozens of dancers explore the dynamics of these eight value systems through sound and movement.

One key outcome was that the above pairs of value systems each ended up having the same basic movements but with a different

Figure 21 : *Spiral Dynamics, Chakras and the iChing*
Newcomb D, personal communication, 2011

quality. The movements in Beige to Blue were more solid and fixed than their echoes in Orange to Turquoise, which were more fluid and relaxed. As we looked into the quality of the energy dynamics related to each worldview pairing, a pattern started to emerge: the outer-systems (starting at beige-turquoise) were more archetypal in their nature, that is to say they reflected more the extremes and essences of yin and yang. The closer you got to the centre, the more refined the systems became, in increasingly subtle combinations of yin and yang. This can be seen in the image, where the white and black circles reflect yin and yang. They are more differentiated in the centre, purer at the extremes.

Seeing Spiral Dynamics in this way gave me the impression that there was somehow a meta-map behind this map, describing the creative process of life, from seed to fruit and back to seed again. I had the image of more subtle archetypal energies coming ever more into form as they move in from the outer dynamics (Beige-Turquoise) to the core, where things crystallise into manifestation (between Blue and Orange). On the Spiral octave map, Blue/Orange is also the location of the heart chakra (verified through body energy research), known to be the ultimate locus of connection and crystallisation.

Performing the movements, I had a sense of a breathing process, out of a field of potential into form and back out again, continually expanding and embracing. It no longer felt linear, but was somehow pulsing in and out, like a heart, connecting energy with matter, or heaven with Earth.

The concept of more subtle layers of reality literally in-forming the physical world reflects Currivan's perspective of The Cosmic Hologram:[18] *"for everything which manifests in the physical world does so as the emergence from deeper and ordered levels of non-physical and in-formed reality."* She notes that everything has a vibrational frequency and wavelength - it is just that energies (in the outer layers of the Spiral) are moving waves whereas particles/matter (at the centre of the Spiral) are *"forms of standing waves"*. Energy and matter are both composed of waves, just differing on a scale of moving or standing. *"The higher the frequency the greater the energy or more fundamentally the information embodied."*

Wilber[19] notes the similar language used to describe the basic realm of physics (which could be seen as the Seed or Level 1 of the volution octave) and the transcendent realm of mysticism (which could be seen as the Potential or Level 8 of the volution octave), a language of interconnectedness outside of linear time and space. Wilber bemoans how this has lead some to conflate the two levels, erroneously suggesting that the realm of Level 1 quantum physics can inform us about Level 8 mysticism.

From a volutionary perspective, we can acknowledge that they are very different stages, while at the same time noting that there is likely to be resonance as these two stages are connected as the outer layer of the torus. Wilber[20] criticises people for suggesting that what Bohm described as *"implicate"* at the physical level could be applied in the same way to the transcendent level. Volution enables us to embrace both perspectives by noting that levels 1 and 8 are indeed very different in their qualities, yet at the same time the creative tension field that they co-create as Seed and Potential is indeed *"implicate"* in the sense that it holds the potential of the manifest reality and is invisible to most people's perception.

The implicate then both *"subscends"* and *"transcends"*[21] visible reality.

The main difference between Wilber's model of vertical stages and the volution thesis, is that Wilber explores only the vertical unfolding, in which an earlier stage holds the implicate order that *"becomes explicate at the next",*[22] whereas volution suggests that there is an implicate to explicate dynamic at work also from the outside of the torus in, through the resonance between polarities of levels in the octave as described above.

This relationship between *"higher"* and *"lower"* meshes with an intuition I have that the more your awareness expands to take in more of reality (e.g. transcendent mysticism) the more refined and differentiated your understanding of the world becomes (e.g. quantum physics).

The transcendence and *"subscendence"* happen in parallel, like a tree having to grow deeper roots to balance higher branches; in that sense, it grows out from the centre. This matches Currivan's description of the life process being one of increasing parallel integration and differentiation.

Small Wright gives this description that matches the volutionary octave:

> *"From our perspective, form and energy create one unit of reality and are differentiated from one another solely by the individual's ability to perceive them with his or her sensory system. In short, the differentiation between form and energy within any given object, plant, animal or human lies with the observer."*[23]

In the volutionary octave, the closer something is to the centre, the more likely we are to be able to perceive its form with our senses. It is ultimately one spectrum of information expressed as energy, which becomes form (as standing waves) at the moment we are able to perceive it. This is reflected in the frequency at which information vibrates, getting lower as it gets denser towards the centre of the torus:

> *"Light vibrates at a frequency of five times 10 to the 14th power Hertz; the Earth's magnetic field vibrates only at 8 to 10 Hertz. Nerve cells can have vibrations between 10 and 1,000 Hertz. Human skin cells vibrate at a frequency of six Hertz."*[24]

I had been exploring the torus for a while as a fundamental pattern of life, but had never really looked into the dynamics that it reflects. What resonated with my inquiry was the subtle, lighter outer skin and denser inner core, mirroring my new sense of Spiral Dynamics. When I saw the animated jitterbug graphic for the first time, I could see before me the breathing process that I had been feeling was related to the dynamic beneath my new Spiral Dynamics map.

The concept of a unified field out of which every form emerges, as described in Chapter 4, resonated with my experience and understanding of there being an absolute and a relative dimension to life. This allowed me to park the absolute perspective with the concept of the unified field, so that I could devote myself to exploring the relative dimension without worrying that I was thereby ignoring the ultimate truth of absolute unity.

The idea of there being a geometry to the unified field, the Vector Equilibrium (VE), which is ready at any moment to come into movement and create form, enabled me to bridge from a feeling of the unified field to a cognitive sense of it in the relative world. It resonated with my understanding of the Spiral Dynamics model having the most fundamental unity-based dynamics at both extremes, holding the other worldview dynamics between two poles. Beige is a sub-conscious pre-cognitive unity system where the drive is pure survival, with no thought process coming between our instinct and its expression, and full living-in-the-moment blending with the environment. This could be seen as the seed.

Turquoise is a supra-conscious post-cognitive unity system that experiences reality as one interlocking sea of energy. This could be seen as the potential. A Vector Equilibrium is six pairs of vectors, six polarities holding the structure in balance.

As I contemplated how this might relate to the Spiral Dynamics octave perspective, I realised that actually only six of the worldviews could be seen to contain polarity, as the extremes of Beige and Turquoise were unity systems. From that perspective, Spiral Dynamics, too, offers a set of six polarity vectors (Purple to Yellow).

I also realised that, in themselves, that set is also in relationship as polarised pairs with Purple-Yellow, Red-Green and Blue-Orange. As I said above, the two members of a pair contain the same basic dynamic, but with a very different form (see opposite):

	Shared Quality	Polarity
Purple-Yellow	Connecting	In-group - All
Red–Green	Identity	Me - We
Blue–Orange	Manifestation	Stable Structure - Growth

These pairs, through their polarity, seem to have the function of pulling potential from the extremes (seed Beige and potential Turquoise) into form at the heart (between Blue and Orange), through the phases of:

- connecting up what needs to be connected and defining what is core and periphery (Purple-Yellow),

- putting it into right relationship by defining the identity of each part and its relationship to the rest (Red-Green),

- and manifesting it in form through creating just enough structure for it to be able to thrive and grow (Blue-Orange).

In geometry, this is known as *"tensional integrity"*, or tensegrity:[25] the tension manifests the form and the form holds the tension.

As I sensed into this dynamic I got an image of the seed (e.g. Beige) and potential (e.g. Turquoise) arising at one and the same moment. This is the moment of conception, following which the subtle energy potential inspires (*"breathes into"*) physical form, which draws down the information through its density and gravity so it can manifest in three-dimensional reality. This includes the passage through the different platonic forms as described in Chapter 4.

In my new understanding of Spiral Dynamics, this process would correlate with the icosahedron being yellow-purple, the dodecahedron green-red and the octahedron blue-orange. A brief review of the qualities of the geometric forms [26] suggests resonance with the worldviews as linked above, although to postulate such with more conviction would need much more research. What we can conclude is that the jitterbug volution dynamic literally links informational potential with material form through its dynamic geometry. This reflects well the Spiral Dynamics model from the perspective I described above. It is the creation process.

Seeing Spiral Dynamics in this way, as an example of a deeper creation dynamic, links it very closely to the dynamics of the torus. The torus describes the form of the flow field surrounding the Vector Equilibrium and jitterbug dynamics. It is essentially a spinning dynamic. As the Vector Equilibrium collapses, the torus form emerges. This connection between the torus and Spiral Dynamics suggests that we can more accurately view the human story in terms of spin, pulses and breath, rather than linear evolution. It was this realisation - that evolution and involution are both part of the core life process, and that neither can exist without the other - that prompted me to use the term *"volution"* instead. When it came to me, I had no idea what it meant, just that it seemed to cover both evolution and involution, being at the root of both. When I looked it up I saw that it meant *"turn"* and *"spin"*, which fits the toroidal perspective.

In Hindu mythology, the cosmos continually regenerates through the non-stop gyration and spin of the God Shiva.[27] Spin is also *"one of the parameters used to describe particles and the one used to test nonlocal correlations between distant particles."*[28] We shall see the relevance of the nonlocal aspect later.

The idea of both an expansion towards the outer, less dense boundaries and a crystallisation towards the centre is reinforced by Currivan: *"As gravity pulls inwards on matter, Dark Energy essentially pushes outwards on space itself."*[29]

Having laid out the argument for revisiting our evolutionary understanding of human development from a volutionary perspective, it is important to note that the linearity still has its place.

From Beige to Blue, our reality manifests in the material plane through the respective worldviews, but each of those systems is in informational resonance with its values-system partner. This could explain why, in the epochs of Beige and Purple (where we were pre-rational in our development), we created great pyramids and temple structures which are today being shown to have encoded in their geometry the physics of the vacuum and so-called *"dark matter."*[30]

The resonance with Turquoise/Yellow somehow enabled Beige/Purple to manifest those structures, bypassing the central cognition-driven value systems (Red to Green). From Orange to Turquoise, our world manifests in resonance with each respective earlier values-system partner, meaning that we have to clear up any pain or unfinished business from the earlier phase to be able to maturely manifest the later one (i.e. orange must fully integrate blue, green must fully integrate red, yellow must fully integrate purple and turquoise must fully integrate beige). This has certainly been my personal experience and would also explain why Dr Don Beck and Ken Wilber targeted a Red-Green combination which they called the Mean Green Meme[31] as a blockage to the emergence of Yellow. The central point of the octave, between Blue and Orange, where we identified the heart chakra in the body-energy research, seems to be where the individual or system becomes conscious of itself and its purpose and goes through a process of integration on its journey to wholeness. The pairs are locked into a co-creative dance. At the end of the process, potential information (heaven) and seed matter (Earth) have been fully fused, all worldviews infuse each other in an octave harmonic, and a major cycle is complete. The toroidal entity is functioning at its highest potential and ready to seed a new scale of manifestation.

Elgin describes what he calls *"dimensional coevolution"* in a similar way:

"Development proceeds as an arc that turns back upon itself. In the initial stages, humanity's evolutionary challenge is to separate from nature and discover our capacities as a relatively autonomous species. In the later stages, our challenge is to reintegrate ourselves with nature

SOCIETY

Establishment of Planetary-Scale Wisdom Civilization (8th D)

Humans acquire the perspective, compassion, and creativity to sustain themselves into the long-term future. A dynamically stable, self-referencing, and self-organizing species-civilization emerges that continually balances between planetary unity and individual, creative diversity.

Era of Balancing Species-Creativity and Unity (7th D)

Planetary civilization moves beyond a concern for maintaining itself to a concern for surpassing itself. The critical challenge is to maintain global unity while coping with the enormous stresses generated by liberating human creativity and diversity. Creative ventures might include the terraforming of Mars and genetic engineering that creates entirely new forms of life.

Era of Global Bonding and Celebration (6th D)

Social compassion becomes the practical basis for organizing a planetary-scale civilization. With a deep sense of bonding and commitment, humanity works to build a sustainable future premised on mutually supportive development. An era of intense cross-cultural learning and global celebration. Much effort is placed on restoring the global environment.

Era of Mass Communication and Global Reconciliation (5th D)

With reflective consciousness realized at a civilizational scale through the creative use of the communications media, humans are able to stand back and cope with the severe ecological stresses generated by the industrial era. With intense local-to-global communication comes reconciliation around a vision for a sustainable future for the earth. The potential for a planetary-scale civilization gains a foothold in human consciousness.

Industrial Era (4th D)

Society is dominated by a materialistic and intellectual worldview. As people perceive the potential for material progress, the mystery of nature gives way to science and the analyzing intellect. Economics of scale in production and an ideological basis for social affiliation combine to foster a nation-state scale of development. Material development becomes the primary measure of social "success" and meaning.

Agricultural Era (3rd D)

A surplus of food makes possible a growing population and the division of labor. The scale of social organization expands from the farming village to the city-state. With a time-sense that recognizes nature's cycles, a settled agrarian existence develops along with supportive forms of civic organization.

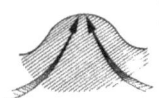

Awakening Hunter-Gatherer Era (2nd D)

Social organization is of limited scale and is influenced by the demands for a mobile existence. With very few possessions there is little basis for material differentiation or conflict. Social affiliation is based upon the tribal group involved in gathering and hunting. Nature is seen as filled with mysterious forces. Magical rituals are developed to harness nature's power.

Archaic Humans (1st D)

With consciousness collapsed into a one-dimensional point, there is no ability to stand back and reflect on self and nature; instead beings are fully embedded within nature and operate largely on automatic. Social organization is extremely limited and extends little beyond the biological family.

Table 5 : *Duane Elgin's Torus Dynamics*   (Elgin 1993, p223)

and to learn to act in conscious harmony with the cosmos. Evolution moves through a nested series of perceptual environments, each with new challenges and potentials, that gradually turn back upon themselves to create self-referencing beings and civilizations that are intimately connected with the deep ecology of the Universe."[32]

Wilber describes how levels in a holarchy like this are *"mutually interpenetrating and interconnecting. But not in an equivalent fashion. The higher transcends but includes the lower - not vice versa."*[33]

He summarises this as a *"multidimensional interpenetration with nonequivalence"*. This means that the higher is aware of, can see and embrace the lower, but not the other way round. Wilber calls the volutionary journey an *"Atman Project"*, referring to the Hindu concept of a World Soul from which all individual souls emerge and to which they return.

Once the initial impulse has been felt and there is a movement out of the unified field, a *"subtle ripple, awakening to itself"*,[34] this ripple wants to return to the Infinite from which it came, yet knows that if it did so it would cease to exist, and is therefore also afraid of returning. Being thus unable to return, it creates all sorts of substitutes, initially setting itself up as a God as it crystallises its own identity, becoming ever denser as it moves from the causal to the subtle to the pranic and the material, where *"it falls into insentient slumber."*[35]

This is the central point of the volution process, where the identity of the entity has fully crystallised, before then becoming more conscious of itself and starting its re-integration towards the next level of wholeness.

Wilber makes an important point that suggests the integration of a more traditional fractal, holographic perspective - as often described in relation to quantum mechanics - with a holarchical understanding of levels or phases as above. He argues that the pure holographic nature of reality can be seen within each level of development, but not across levels.

The physicists discovered holograms in the physical realm, a *"one dimensional interpenetration of the material plane"*, [36] where all elements of that realm are *"mutually interpenetrating and interdependent"*.

However, the nature of the holographic patterns at that level are not the same as the patterns at a different level, for example biological, mental or pranic. This means we need to talk about a holographic holarchical reality, in which patterns will exist between the levels but the patterns within each level cannot be reduced to the patterns within another level.

Given that it is all information expressed in different ways, the informational imprint will exist across levels, yet it will express itself differently within each level. Wilber argues this strongly, in order to discourage a growing trend of immediately assuming that patterns found at the quantum physical level can be applied to the subtle and causal levels.

An overlap of language adds to the confusion (e.g. interconnectedness, oneness) but it is important to distinguish between a pre-conscious experience of unity (e.g. Spiral Dynamics beige or quantum mechanics) and a post-conscious experience of unity (e.g. Spiral Dynamics Turquoise or transcendent consciousness).

Frank Barr, in his description of Arthur M Young's work, describes a similar process, where manifestation starts with the Potential (Seed) at level 1 and then descends into form and connection before returning conscious to level 1 as *"realisation".*

Figure 22 : *Reflexive 7-Staged Arc of Arthur M Young*

In this case the pivot moment and level 4 would be equivalent to the two related phases in the voluntionary octave. Arthur M. Young also mapped his seven phases onto the geometry of a torus.

Anne Baring[37] describes our civilisation's journey from the lunar to the solar to the integration of solar and lunar. The phases of development that Baring describes can be related to the eight Spiral Dynamics stages in the following way:

- **Beige/Purple** - lunar instinctive; the time we are immersed in lunar consciousness without being aware of there being a potentially different way of experiencing life.

- **Red/Blue** - solar instinctive; the time we grow into solar consciousness as a reaction to the limitations of the lunar age, unaware of the potential implications of our solar impulse.

- **Orange/Green** - solar integration; the time we become aware of our solar development:

  Orange becomes aware of Blue rules and structure and we learn to play the game; Green becomes aware of Red individuality and diversity so looks to embrace it.

- **Yellow/Turquoise** - lunar integration; as we become aware of the lunar parts of ourselves that we left behind a while ago, and are confronted by the limits of our solar development:

  Yellow becomes aware of Purple interconnectedness, so seeks to re-integrate everything;

  Turquoise becomes aware of Beige unity and body-instinct consciousness, so looks to engage it consciously and complete the cycle.

From Seed to Potential

This awareness helped me to develop a basic map of the volutionary development from seed to potential.

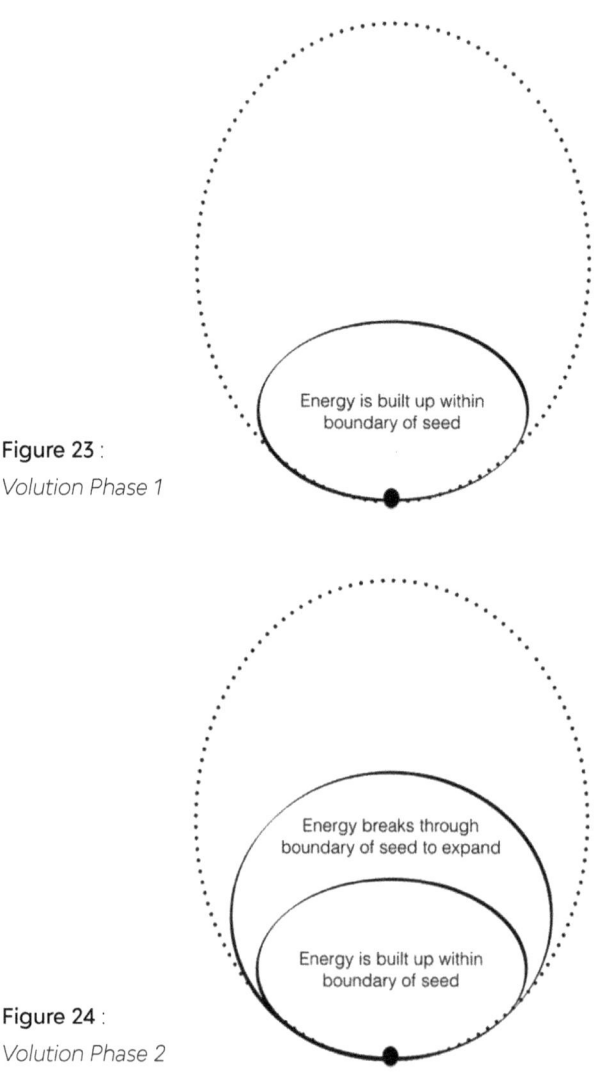

Figure 23 :

Volution Phase 1

Figure 24 :

Volution Phase 2

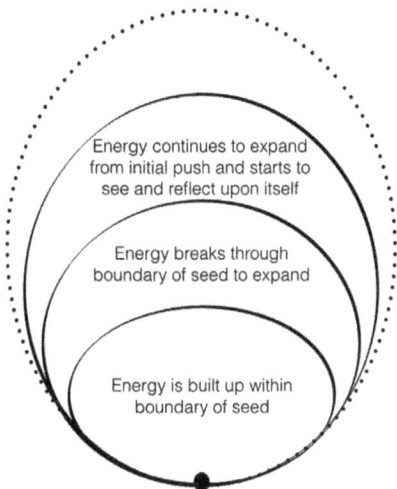

Figure 25 :

Volution Phase 3

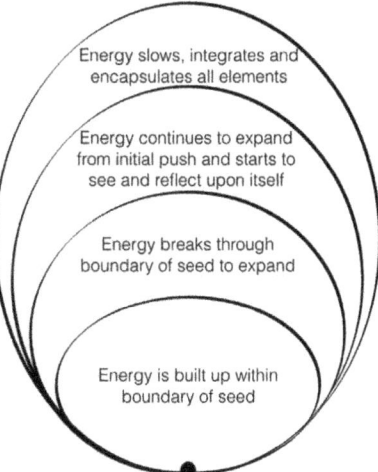

Figure 26 :

Volution Phase 4

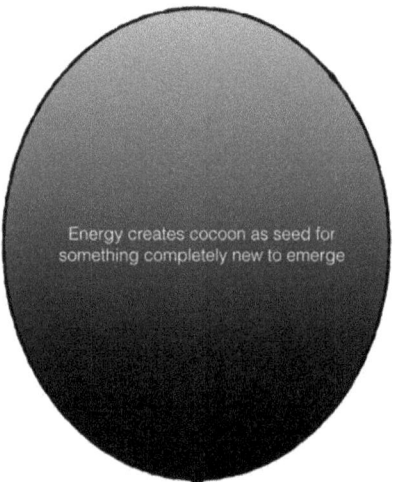

Figure 27 :
Volution Phase 5

Relating the Lunar-Solar-Integration phases to this description would look as follows:

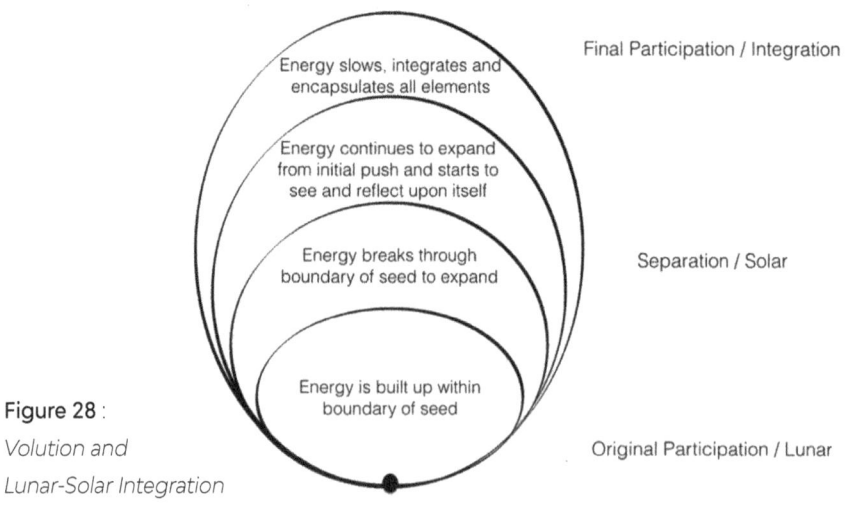

Figure 28 :
Volution and
Lunar-Solar Integration

Expand and Embrace

With this perspective, we now return to the seeming mirror-like dynamic whereby the system develops to a moment of self-awareness (through the first four phases in the octave model), and then consciously sets about integrating the earlier developed parts of itself, as each of the subsequent four phases becomes a conscious expression of its earlier partner system.*

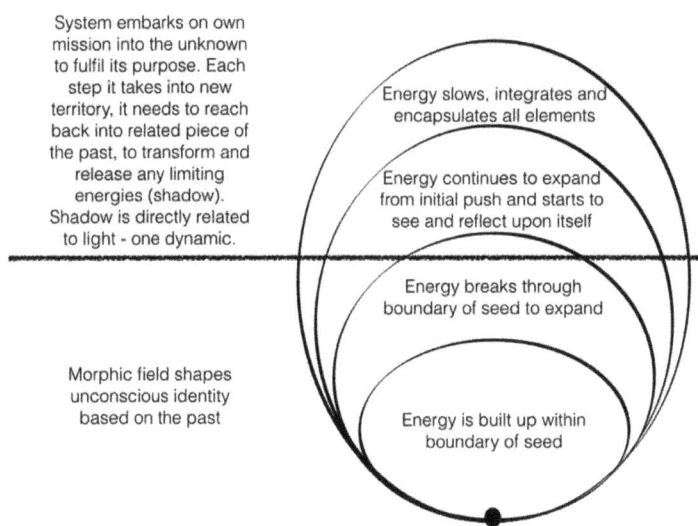

Figure 29 : *Two Major Phases of Volution*

---

* It may well be that the "halfway point" between levels 4 and 5 is actually a golden ratio proportion of 1:1,618 as compared to literally half way (see previous sections).

Arthur M. Young also mapped his seven phases onto the geometry of a torus.

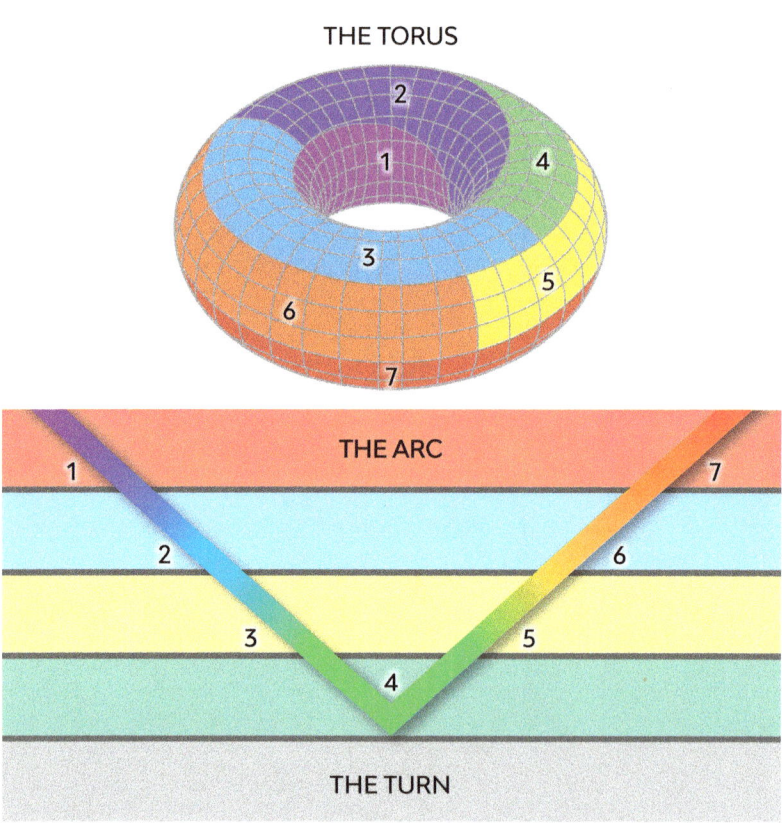

Figure 30 : *Arthur M. Young's 7 Reflexive Stages mapped to the Torus*
Source: Foster Gamble

Currivan[38] describes this central *"crossover"* point in the life of our Universe:

"From the outward push of the Big Bang, the expansion of space slowly decelerated due to the gravitational effect of both visible and Dark Matter enabling both to cluster into stars and galaxies. But as space extends beyond a certain point, the density of such attractive energies diminishes until a crossover is reached with the density of Dark Energy, which then dominates over the remaining life-time of our Universe."

In this description we see a shift at the crossover point from the domination of Dark Matter to the domination of Dark Energy. In volution language, Dark Matter can be seen as the equivalent of the seed energy and Dark Energy as the equivalent of the potential energy.

For the first part of the journey the past patterns dominate that are held in the seed, and for the second the future patterns dominate that are held in the potential.

Walter Russell saw these two dynamics continually going on in parallel:

"The essence of the wave can be expressed as the appearance and disappearance of motion/matter from the One in two directions: direction from the inertial, cathode plane and its progression through four generating stages to maturity at the anode where it simulates stillness in the One by fast motion, and then from there in the other direction through four degenerating stages to dissolution where it again loses form in the inertial, cathode plane, stillness. The one aspect of motion common to both these directions is spiral motion."[39]

Here we can picture the spiral motion of the torus pulling into more dense form at the centre where the dense boundaries increase the speed of the component parts and higher frequency standing wave forms, to the extent that it appears to be still - and then the expansion out to the outer boundaries where it is also still, but this time due to the space. So the boundaries and core of the torus are an experience of opposite kinds of stillness, with the spiralling dynamics bridging the space in between.

From a linear perspective, for the first half of that journey the entity is relatively unconscious of itself and is following a pathway of development that is more shaped from its environment than from its own internal will. The first half of the journey draws on pre-existing information captured from the past experiences of similar entities, information that is held in information fields, such as Sheldrake's morphogenetic fields [40] or Laszlo's Akashic field. [41]

These fields hold archetypal patterns that go on to influence how the system manifests. The system only becomes aware of these patterns in the later stages of the second half of the journey. [42] These archetypal patterns provide an invisible level of coherence underlying the increasingly differentiated and seemingly chaotic manifest expression. In this first half of the journey, the entity is 'downloading'. past patterns from that field and acting without much initiative or free will of its own - in much the same way that collectives such as organisations do when they are running on auto-pilot with little innovation (this is described in detail in Senge et al [43] and labelled as *"downloading"*).

For the second half of the journey, the entity is waking up to itself, realising that it has choices about its existence and starting to co-create reality rather than simply consume reality as it is. However, in order to move forward in that way, and add new information to the fields, or create new *"kosmic grooves"*, as Ken Wilber[44] would call them, energy that is held within the system linked to past experiences and beliefs needs to be transformed and released.

From this perspective, an entity adheres to the law of the conservation of energy: the total energy of an isolated system remains constant and is said to be conserved over time. From the moment of seed-potential conception, the system has all the energy it needs to manifest its potential. In order to evolve beyond the way things have been until the present, though, the entity needs to transform and release old energy to co-create new expressions of life. New insights - new light - reveals new shadows that need integrating to manifest the potential of the new awareness.

In the context of this seemingly intricate relationship between the past and the future, it is interesting to note that the term *"uvatiarru"*, used by the Inuit of Baffin Island, can be translated as both *"long ago"* and *"in the future."*[45] In the introduction to her poetic work about this process, Rees describes this second half of the journey as "the recovery of memory."[46]

This process was at the heart of the work of CG Jung. In Memories, Dreams, Reflections, he begins his Prologue with these words:

"My life is a story of the self-realisation of the unconscious. Everything in the unconscious seeks outward manifestation, and the personality too desires to evolve out of its unconscious conditions and to experience itself as a whole." [47]

Later on in the same work he reaches the conclusion that *"there is no linear evolution; there is only a circumambulation of the self."*[48] That looks very much like Figure 31 opposite, where the self at the centre goes through a process of expanding and embracing.

The process of transforming past energy for new futures can be described in five phases:

1. An impulse to growth - the entity feels the pull to develop a new part of its potential.

2. Light descends - this impulse releases new information or the light of awareness into the entity.

3. Shadow enlightened - the patterns of the past that need transforming are revealed.

4. Energy released - energy is released as the past patterns are transformed.

5. Growth - with the new energy, the entity is able to crystallise and embody the new information, accessing new degrees of freedom.

The light of the new information triggers an expansive drive for greater agency and freedom, while at the same time love and understanding are needed to embrace and integrate the past. These two fundamental dynamics, that happen in parallel to each other, reflect two of the main drives of a holon (figure 31) as described by Wilber:[49] agency and communion.

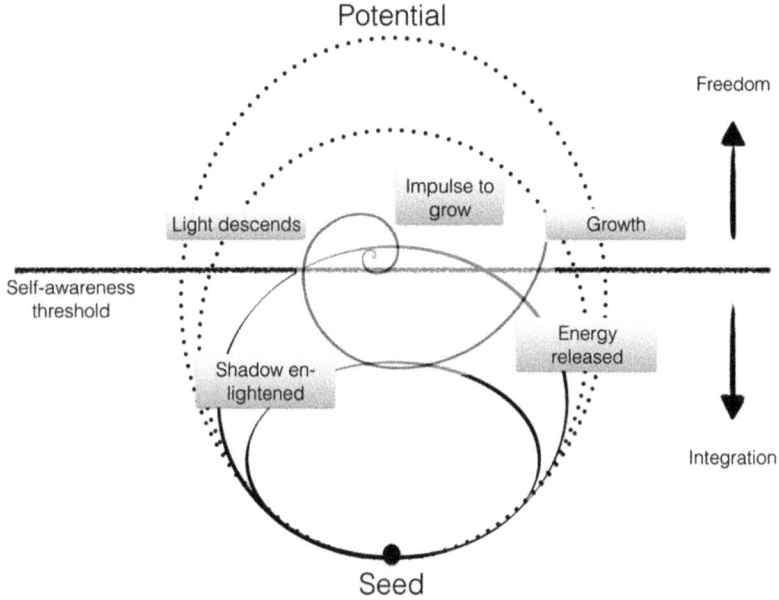

Figure 31 : *The Volutionary Journey of Integration and Freedom*

This equates to three energies: stretching for the light, reconnecting with love, and being at the centre between the two, which could be seen as an expression of the three personal perspectives of language. Reaching out to something outside of us (an *"it"*) is a third person expression; reconnecting with love to past trauma to put humpty dumpty back together again is engaging in a relationship with a second person *"you"* to make a *"we"*; while the first person *"I"* sits at the centre of this dynamic. In this way the three personal perspectives can be seen as part of the dynamic volution of life, not simply as categories of perspective.

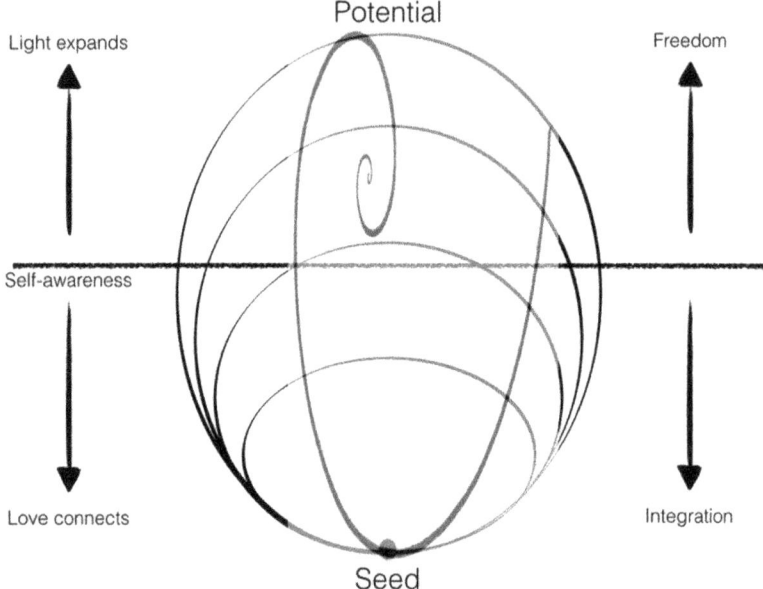

Figure 32 : *The Role of Light and Love in Volution*

To release the information for greater agency, the sub-holons that currently make up the main holon need to be re-arranged so they become more efficient, leaving more energy for growth through more natural communion. The relationships of the parts to each other and to the whole grow increasingly close to natural proportions as they crystallise into greater refinement, thus needing less energy themselves and releasing more for further growth and agency of the whole.*

Currivan beautifully summarises this process of healing and completion: *"whilst in its rising and falling the polarity expressions of yang and yin are overt, it is in the turning points of its peaking and reforming that the cycle is able to complete and move on."*[50]

Another perspective on the process of reaching down to heal past trauma in order to release the information for future development can be found in the change model of Spiral Dynamics.[51] A fundamental element of the Spiral Dynamics model is the understanding of how value systems change.

CHANGE VARIATIONS		
CV-8	*Quantum Change*	change occurs at every level, across whole system
CV-7	*Up-shift*	evolutionary change up to the next level of complexity
CV-6	*Break-out*	barriers of old order are removed (more or less aggressively)
CV-5	*Up-stretch*	current state temporarily stretches to include some more complexity
CV-4	*Down-stretch*	temporary regression to access earlier, less complex coping systems
CV-3	*Upgrade*	basic system remains the same, with improvement in functioning
CV-2	*Reform*	elements remain the same, but are re-aligned to meet same objectives
CV-1	*Fine-tune*	Make simple adjustments to fit function better

Table 6 : *Spiral Dynamics Change Variations*
(Beck & Cowan 1996)

---

* The *"natural proportions"* are related to a *"golden mean"* found in nature, as in the Fibonnacci sequence and the proportion referred to as *"Phi"*.

The change model comprises three main parts: a description of states of change (from stable through transition phases into new stability), a description of the conditions that need to be in place for change to happen, and a description of different types of change known as change variations. These three are connected through a powerful change matrix. For this point, I am going to focus first on the change variations. These describe different intensities of change that a system can experience:

CV-4, the *"down-stretch"* is related to the going back to heal past pain while the CV-5 *"up-stretch"* accesses more light and information from a potential future. We cannot shift into the *"vertical"* change dynamics of change variations 6-8, where the whole system renews, until we have done enough down- and up-stretching. The down-stretching will release energy locked in past traumas, and the up-stretching will access new, higher frequency energy of the future. It is this build up of energy that pushes us into the break-out and up-shift when the time is ripe.

People's ability to influence the past, too, has been demonstrated through experiments. Radin[52] documents what he calls a *"time-reversed, or retrocausal, experiment"* that demonstrated how people exerting a certain intention three months after data was originally recorded had an influence on that previously recorded data.

This implies that the past is not fixed and can be influenced from its future. The key seems to be when the observation happens, which is always in the present. In this case, *"the observation phase... took place three months after the data were generated and recorded."*

So although recorded at the start point by a computer, they were not consciously observed by a human being until three months later. The observer cannot be separated from the observed. In a personal communication, Dr Radin commented:

"The results of these "retro" experiments do not mean that previously recorded data were changed, because without knowing for sure what was already recorded (by observing it) we can't tell if it had been changed or not. Thus, what we can say is that data recorded in the past was later found to be in alignment with future instructions to mentally influence those data. i.e., the past cannot be changed after the fact, but it can be influenced as it occurs, from the future." [53]

Informational Entropy

This process of development whereby differentiation increases over time is the dynamics of informational entropy. In The Cosmic Hologram, Currivan[54] describes entropy in terms of informational content and flow (see also Laszlo & Currivan).[55] The term 'entropy' is often used to refer to the relative measure of order or disorder in a system, with increasing entropy being related to increasing disorder, although physicists actually understand it as a difference in the microstates of the system, from simplicity to complexity (see for example Boltzmann).[56] The dynamics of entropy are captured in the Second Law of Thermodynamics, which states that: 'The entropy of an isolated system will always tend to stay the same or to increase.'

From a volutionary perspective, entropy is at its lowest, as it was just before the Big Bang, at the seed-potential initiation moment. In other words, order is at its greatest and everything is undifferentiated in the seed, with the potential being held in the informational field. As the process of life and manifestation unfolds, the information and seed grow into each other. The seed expands and differentiates into increasing numbers of parts, at the same time as the brane of the entity expands with the increasing differentiation of the information it holds (as described above).

Entropy increases as the original undifferentiated unity and order becomes increasingly expressed in a diversity of form and *"disorder"*. This is literally what creates our experience of linear time.[57] Towards the centre of the volutionary torus, information gains mass as the energy forms into standing waves, and *"mass slows things down... enabling the entropic flow of information and so the experience of time itself"*. It is important to note that the increase in entropy and *"disorder"* does not mean that the parts lose their interconnectedness - they are still held together by the field of the entity as a whole, being simply diverse expressions of that one original impulse. This use of the term 'entropy' is different to the way in which it is often used simply to mean breakdown. Wilber[58] distinguishes between *"agape"*, which is the embrace of the parts and fits informational entropy, and *"thanatos"*, which is a breakdown into parts which lose their interrelatedness.

Out of the increasing *"disorder"* of informational entropy, a new level of order starts to emerge. This emergence of a new order has been called *"syntropy"* or *"negentropy"*. According to Griffith,[59] biologists use the latter term to describe the basic direction of life, with increasing cooperation. The Wikipedia entry on negentropy notes that *"In 2009, Mahulikar & Herwig redefined negentropy of a dynamically ordered sub-system as the specific entropy deficit of the ordered sub-system relative to its surrounding chaos."* Given that the volutionary impulse is a response to a need in the world, the *"surrounding chaos"* is context which the entity is growing in response to. So *"entropy deficit"* is when the entity has not yet differentiated into the degree of diversity required to deal with the level of complexity of the life conditions in which it finds itself. Negentropy, then, is the entity's relative ability to deal with the complexity of its life conditions - it is the emerging order of the mature entity that it is becoming.

Currivan[60] notes that there is actually no need to create other terms alongside entropy (such as syntropy or negentropy), as informational entropy covers the whole process of increasing parallel differentiation and reintegration. Just as volution is a single process comprising involution and evolution, so entropy is a single process of information expressed as space-time. It moves from simplicity to complexity concentrated in greater differentiation. In the volution model, the Seed Potential field represents information expressed as matter-energy, which is conserved, in accordance with quantum theory on energy matter and its conservation.

The integration of the Seed with its Potential is information expressed entropically, going from minimum entropy to its maximum entropy, in accordance with relativity theory on space-time and the second law of thermodynamics. Traditionally, scientists have struggled to reconcile quantum theory with relativity theory, since they have appeared to be in conflict. Currivan simply refers to them, respectively, as the first law of information and the second law of information. Together they are a perfect way to make a Universe.

Currivan[61] has framed it as follows: the First Law of Thermodynamics - that *"energy-matter, whilst changing its forms, is universally conserved"* - transforms to the *"First Law of Information: Information expressed as energy-matter, whilst changing its forms, is symmetrically and universally conserved throughout our Universal lifecycle - essentially Quantum Theory".*

The Second Law of Thermodynamics namely *"entropy can only increase"* becomes the *"Second Law of Information: Information expressed as space-time can only asymmetrically and entropically increase throughout our Universal lifecycle - essentially Relativity Theory".*

Key is also that within any bounded system, the amount of energy is conserved throughout its life process, with the expansive and attractive forces in balance.[62] Therefore, any energy trapped in earlier stages of the system needs to be released in order for the system to complete its journey to new wholeness.

In the volution model, the original order has the greatest influence on the system until the halfway point is reached in its development, when the new order starts to dominate: the process shifts from a pull from the past to a pull from the future. At its highest level of differentiation or *"disorder"* (as compared with the original order), the system is actually at its most ordered in terms of the entity that it was born to become - the fruit of the seed that becomes a new seed.

According to Dylan Newcomb's work, that continues to relate these kinds of dynamics to the I Ching, in the second half of the octave cycle, the system has a foundational pro-active energy, as compared to a reactive foundation in the first half.[63]

This reinforces the argument that the system becomes more self-aware once it passes the half-way point and pro-actively starts to co-create its reality rather than simply *"downloading"* pre-existing patterns in the information fields.

Newcomb also notes the increasing degrees of *"sophistication and freedom"* as an entity matures, together with an increasing ability to deal with complexity with less conflict and to hold a longer timespan in its awareness. These last two points reflect the same characteristics of the Spiral Dynamics value systems as they unfold - in fact, Graves[64] said that all he could tell about the general directionality of the value systems was their increasing ability to deal with complexity.

Newcomb also sees this as increasing entropy and relates it to increasing asymmetry, as described in the work of Tom Bearden and Michael Leyton.[65] Bearden seems to be pointing to the same process using different terms, where *"symmetry"* would relate to *"order"* and *"asymmetry"* to *"disorder"*, both describing an entropic process of increasing differentiation leading to the emergence of a new level of order.

When Newcomb analyses the I Ching hexagrams he sees each yáo (broken or unbroken horizontal line) as reflecting the increasing maturity of a system, moving from the base of the hexagram up. Newcomb sees the top trigram as the *"context"* and the lower trigram as the *"action"*, with the two integrating with each other in the same octave dynamic as described above.

The entity thus grows to become mature enough to deal adequately with its context, at which point it reaches fruition. Given the amount of information now in the system, it needs to emerge into a new form and let go of the old, so that it can continue the process of informational entropy, absorbing more information and differentiating into ever more refined and interconnected expressions of life.

Currivan describes this moment of fruition in the life, and projected death, of our Universe:

> *"...perhaps like a bubble that bursts as its inner pressure equals that of the surrounding atmosphere, this end-time may express a point*

of equivalence when our Universe may release its accumulated information, knowledge and wisdom into the infinite Cosmic plenum within which it was born, lives and will die."[66]

If this process is extended to any entity, we could say that once the volutionary octave process is complete, and the original impulse for that manifestation of life has run its course, then the *"inner pressure"* of the seed-potential now matches the *"surrounding atmosphere"* of the life conditions it has entered into to fill a niche, reaching "equivalence" and dissolving itself into the bigger whole, making all its information and wisdom available, thereby seeding new possibilities.

One could say that the mission given to this entity by the greater life process of the system it is part of - a mission to bring certain information into the system - has been successfully completed and the entity's final act is to gift that information to the system as a whole.

Elgin[67] describes this process in a similar way, marking the turning point as the moment we achieve *"self-referencing knowing - when we 'know that we know'"*. This is the same as the mid-point in the volutionary process. From that point on, he believes, *"we no longer require the density of our material world and physical body to centre our knowing process upon itself"*. The body can then die and the entity endures "as a subtle body of light and knowing."

Teilhard de Chardin describes this completion moment as the *"Omega point"*. Brian Swimme[68] summarises it in this way: *"The Universe is moving in the direction of reaching a point where every aspect of the Universe knows every other aspect in its depth."* This reflects the volutionary moment where the whole system is fully integrated and conscious of itself.

Walter Russell sees the process as ongoing rather than linear, *"a steady explosion and implosion state of eternal creation, a continuous life-and-death cycling... It is a two-way, continuous-creation, eternally living-dying Universe."*[69]

This volutionary process also matches the dynamics of holons and holarchies described by Wilber, which we touched on in the previous section. Wilber identifies four *"fundamental capacities"* of holons:[70] self-preservation (a capacity *"to preserve their own particular wholeness or autonomy"*), self-adaptation (a capacity *"to adapt or accommodate itself to other holons"*), self-transcendence (a capacity for *"transformation that results in something novel and emergent"*), and self-embrace (*"Agape reaches down and embraces all the lower holons in the higher holon"*[71]). The process I describe above focuses primarily on the self-transcendence and self-embracing capacities, which go hand-in-hand with *"symmetry breaks"* (Wilber quoting Jantsch) - a break down of the original order so that a new order can emerge. In that process, Wilber refers to Whitehead's famous dictum *"The many become one and are increased by one."*[72] The differentiation that emerges with the increased entropy comes together again in a new unity which adds a new level of complex life. In that new order, the old is *"transcended but included"*, and comes into a greater level of order so that it can be of more coherent service to the new whole.

Wilber quotes the biologist Rupert Sheldrake on this matter: *"The morphic units in isolation behave more indeterminately when they are part of a higher level morphic unit. The higher level morphogenetic field restricts and patterns their intrinsic indeterminism."*[73]

The higher level brane increases the probability of the lower level branes acting in ways to support the purpose of the higher level system. Wilber's final major tenet on holarchies (*"Evolution has directionality"*) summarises that directionality with five main aspects: increasing complexity, increasing differentiation/integration, increasing organisation/structuration, increasing relative autonomy and increasing telos.[74]

The volution model as described above shows how a more expanded brane with more information is able to deal with greater complexity. Differentiation/integration is the informational entropic process. The increasing organisation happens as new levels of brane emerge to contain a larger number of sub-branes. The increasing relative autonomy is related to the increasing ability of a more expanded brane to deal with greater complexity (*"a holon's capacity for self-preservation in the midst of environmental fluctuations."*[75] Wilber describes increasing telos as the *"chaotic attractor"* (referring to Chaos Theory) that is pulling the system towards a new level of order out of the increasing differentiation and apparent chaos.

In the volution model, the chaotic attractors would start to exert their greatest pull past the half-way point in the life-cycle, whereas during the first half of the journey the behaviour of the entity is dominated by the existing *"periodic attractors"* of the old stable system. It is worth quoting Laszlo at length on this:

> *"When growing fluctuations upset the dynamic stability of a system, its stable point of periodic attractors can no longer maintain it in its established state; chaotic attractors appear and with them an interval of transition hallmarked by transitory chaos. When the system achieves a new state of dynamic stability, the chaotic attractors of the bifurcation epoch give way to a new set of point or periodic attractors.*
>
> *"These attractors maintain the system in a condition far from thermodynamic equilibrium, with more effective use of information, greater efficiency in the use of free energies, greater flexibility, as well as greater structural complexity on a higher level of organisation."*[76]

In this Chapter we have looked at evidence for certain stages of development and dynamics within the volution process, completing the theoretical description of volution. In the next section we will look at the implications of applying this perspective to individual, cultural and societal development.

---

[1] *Currivan, The Wave (2005) p52*

[2] *Currivan, The Wave (2005) p52*

[3] *Currivan, The Wave (2005) p52-53*

[4] *Currivan, The Wave (2005) p82*

5   *Currivan, The Wave (2005) p230*

6   *Elgin (1993) p206*

7   *Elgin (1993) p218*

8   *Elgin (1993) p207*

9   *Timothy Leary (1987)*

10 *Dylan Newcomb (personal communication, 10 May 2016)*

11 *Beck & Cowan (1996)*

12 *Dr Clare W Graves (2002)*

13 *Wilber (1996), Cohen (2011), Laszlo (1996)*

14 *Merry (2009)*

15 *Beck & Cowan, Spiral Dynamics (1996)*

16 *Wilber (1996)*

17 *Dr Clare W Graves (2002)*

18 *Currivan's perspective of The Cosmic Hologram (2017)*

19 *Wilber (1982) p166-168*

20 *Wilber (1982) p168*

21 *Wilber (1982) p168*

22 *Wilber (1982) p171*

23 *Small Wright (1997) p3*

24 *Nefiodow (2014) p106*

25 *Edmondson, A (2009)*

26 *Patinkas (2014)*

27 *Elgin (1993) p285*

28 *Hardy (2008)*

29 *Currivan (2017)*

30 *Melchizedek (1990)*

31 *Wilber (2003)*

32 *Elgin (1993) p220*

33 *Wilber (1982) p160*

34 *Wilber (1982) p161*

[35] *Wilber (1982) p161*

[36] *Wilber (1982) p164*

[37] *Anne Baring (2013)*

[38] *Currivan (2017)*

[39] *Binder (1995) p48*

[40] *Sheldrake's morphogenetic fields (1981)*

[41] *Laszlo's Akashic field (2004)*

[42] *Grof (2012)*

[43] *Senge et al (2004)*

[44] *Ken Wilber (1995)*

[45] *Abram (1996) p221*

[46] *Rees (2013) p12*

[47] *CG Jung, Memories, Dreams, Reflections (1995) p17*

[48] *CG Jung, Memories, Dreams, Reflections (1995) p222*

[49] *Wilber (2005)*

[50] *Currivan (2005) p35*

[51] *Beck & Cowan (1996)*

[52] *Radin (2013) p263-265*

[53] *Dr Dean Radin (personal communication, 6th March 2020)*

[54] *Currivan, The Cosmic Hologram, (2017)*

[55] *Laszlo & Currivan (2008) p49*

[56] *Boltzmann (1866)*

[57] *Laszlo & Currivan (2008) p54-55*

[58] *Wilber (personal communication, 24th September 2016)*

[59] *Griffith (2011)*

[60] *Currivan (personal communication, 11th February 2016)*

[61] *Currivan (2016)*

[62] *Currivan (2017) p27*

[63] *D. Newcomb (personal communication, 15th December 2015)*

[64] *Graves (2002)*

[65] *Tom Bearden and Michael Leyton (2003)*

[66] *Currivan (2017) p39*

[67] *Elgin (1993) p301*

[68] *Brian Swimme (1990)*

[69] *Walter Russell, Binder (1995) p45*

[70] *Wilber (1995) p40-46*

[71] *Wilber (personal communication, 24th September 2016)*

[72] *Wilber (1995) p49*

[73] *Wilber (1995) p54*

[74] *Wilber (1995) p67-78*

[75] *Wilber (1995) p71*

[76] *Laszlo (1994) p93*

Chapter Five :
Volution in the Individual, Culture and Society

The Thesis: *This volutionary perspective can be applied to human individual, cultural and societal development.*

This chapter looks at the implications of the volutionary perspective for both the individual and the collective, starting with the individual level, within the context of the collective. The first part looks at how the birth and development process relates to the volution model described above, and how it informs a fundamental aspect of the current planetary challenges.

Incarnation and Separation

"O friend, understand: the body
is like the ocean,
rich with hidden treasures.

"Open your inmost chamber and light its lamp.

"Within the body are gardens,
rare flowers, peacocks, the inner music;
within the body a lake of bliss,
on it the white soul-swans take their joy.

And in the body, a vast market –
go there, trade,
sell yourself for a profit you can't spend.

"Mira says, her Lord is beyond praising.
Allow her to dwell near Your feet."

Mirabai, in Harvey[1]

The volution thesis has been informed, among other things, by explorations around the nature of the apparent split between humanity and the pre-cognitive experience of being one with the Earth, the sensory world and the body.

Healing the perception of this split is key to navigating our current collective crisis.[2] It will also give access to the trans-cognitive consciousness from which it is possible to work more effectively and gracefully with the energetic and informational aspects of life.

This transition is framed using the theory of Spiral Dynamics in Figure 33. In this conception the pain is where the split lies and is due to people forgetting their identity as an expression of the Earth as our physical beings, as well as part of a bigger cosmic wholeness.

When we incarnate out of oneness, we must forget the oneness or we would be unable to be really present in the relative world. We are like actors stepping into a role.

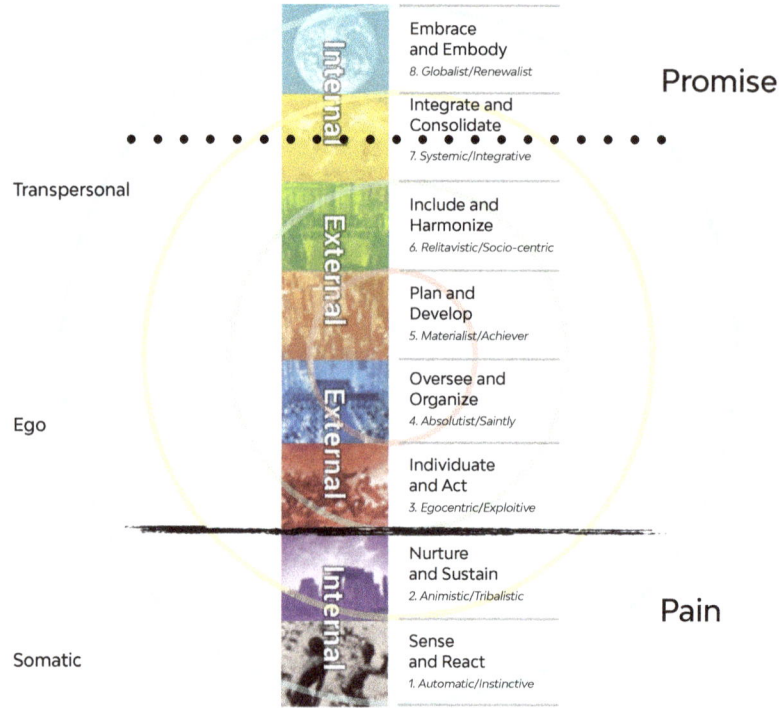

Figure 33 : *The Pain and the Promise through the Spiral Dynamics Lens*

Yet somewhere we miss that oneness, and that missing creates great emotional angst. The promise lies in being granted access to the wholeness of the trans-personal realms as the apparent split is healed. Taegel[3] notes that *"Jean Gebser argues for a retrieval of those qualities from the inner being that reach back to the archaic, the primordial mind".* That *"reaching back"* is to the earliest phases of our development, linked to our body and biology.

In Genesis two trees are described, the tree of knowledge and the tree of life. When people eat of the tree of knowledge they are prevented from accessing the tree of life by cherubims and a flaming sword.

This reflects the story of the split. Our rational mind cannot access the volutionary torus that generates all life. They are seen, at the stage of the split, as mutually exclusive so that rationality, based on separation, cannot twist and corrupt the power of the life force. We have to heal the split, or *"the fall"*, before we are given access to the *"powers of co-creation."*[4]

Jahn and Dunne refer to research by the French biologist Rene Peo'ch which demonstrated how a group of baby chicks influenced the behaviour of a randomly driven robot. They concluded:

> *"The capacity of these animals to affect the trajectory of the robot to their biological advantage by some anomalous means lends credence to the hypothesis that we may be dealing with a phenomenon that is fundamentally biological in nature."*[5]

Jahn and Dunne suggest that such experiments *"might be evidence of the life force itself–what French philosopher Henri Bergson spoke of as the élan vital that underlies the creation of all living things."*[6] This reinforces the argument that if we are to be able to access that kind of influence consciously, we need to heal our relationship to our body and our earliest stages of development.

CG Jung describes this split as the source of much of the neuroticism that he experienced in his day:

> *"Among the so-called neurotics of our day there are a good many who in other ages would not have been neurotic – that is, divided*

against themselves. If they had lived in a period and in a milieu in which man was linked by myth with the world of the ancestors, and thus with nature truly experienced and not merely seen from outside, they would have been spared this division within themselves."[7]

Later on he connects that to the collective condition:

"It is precisely the loss of connection with the past, our uprootedness, which has given rise to the "discontents" of civilisation and to such a flurry and haste that we live more in the future and its chimerical promises of the golden age than in the present, with which our whole evolutionary background has not yet caught up."[8]

A sentence in Grof's Healing our Deepest Wounds[9] broadens this perspective: *"Although the process of incarnation separates and alienates us from our source, the awareness of this fact is never completely lost."* This points to incarnation as a process, and that process of coming into ever more crystalline form goes hand-in-hand with an increasing experience of alienation from our state of prior unity.

The process of incarnation can then be seen as one where our soul chooses to leave the unity awareness in which it resides between lives, to incarnate, co-create and learn any lessons that it has to learn, as testified to by many who have experienced near-death experiences.[10] Spangler describes it this way: *"The soul intentionally turns part of itself into a state of consciousness and a form that can manifest and function in a physical environment like the Earth."[11]*

Once it starts its journey from the unity field, it becomes ever denser energy as it manifests as the baby in the womb and continues to refine and crystallise its form until it reaches a level of density from which it starts the return to the unity field. This moment may be well into adult life. In the Kybalion[12] this process is described as the *"outpouring"*, where *"the All"* pours out unindividualised energy, vibrations get lower and lower until the urge ceases and then the return begins with the *"indrawing"* to *"the All"* as multiple individualised units of life through evolution and increasingly subtle energetic vibration.

From this perspective, the split that is identified above is just one of many stages in the incarnation and separation process. While it is a key one, particularly for our current planetary condition, it nevertheless changes the perspective to see it as one phase in a broader incarnation process.

Abram describes this healing through the integration of space and time, which from his perspective have been split off from each other, I would argue, as part of the same process described above.

"The conceptual separation of time and space–the literate distinction between linear, progressive time and homogenous, featureless space–functions to eclipse the enveloping Earth from human awareness. As long as we structure our lives according to assumed parameters of a static space and a rectilinear time, we will be able to ignore, or overlook, our thorough dependence upon the Earth around us. Only when space and time are reconciled into a single,

unified field of phenomena does the encompassing Earth become evident, once again, in all its power and its depth, as the very ground and horizon of all our knowing."[13]

From the body-mind research I carried out with Dylan Newcomb, where we took the Spiral Dynamics model as a starting point for creating a new understanding of the life process, the incarnation and densifying process happens up until the middle of the octave of eight energy dynamics (i.e. between *"Blue"* and *"Orange"*), after which point

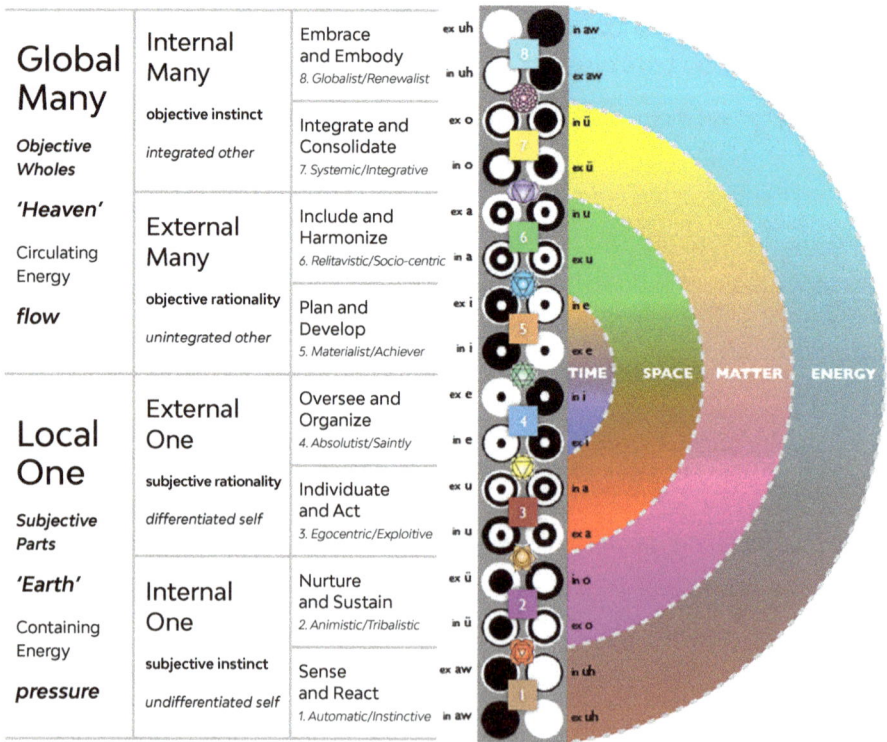

Figure 34 : *Fractal Patterns in a Volutionary Octave*

the return to unity begins as the mind starts to expand into the space beyond the personality that it formed, thus expanding its sense of identity from more ego-centric, to world- and kosmo-centric.[14]

This is illustrated in Figure 34 in Newcomb's image with the labels on the left, as the perspective shifts at the mid-point of the octave from *"local"* to *"global"* and from *"one"* to *"many"*, ending in an internalisation of the other as we return to identifying ourselves as a unity with the world around us.

The Return to Unity Awareness

"At one time they grew to be one alone from being many, and at another they grew apart again to be many from being one."

Empedocles, in Harvey[15]

A teleseries with Stanislav Grof and friends[16] repeatedly emphasised that humanity's current transition has much to do with a re-integration of the more feminine, yin qualities. Grof noted that a significant group in the population was shifting *"to a sense of fundamental embeddedness in Nature."* The same teleseries quoted both Paul Ray's work pointing to the emergence of the Cultural Creatives (a large segment in Western society, in particular, that has developed beyond the standard paradigm of Modernists versus Conservatives) and their more feminine values.[17]

New *"yin economics"* was referenced, pointing to the rise of complementary currencies that emphasise collaboration rather than competition. These expressions all seem to point to the more fundamental shift underway, as described above: the reintegration of yin in the co-creative sacred marriage and dynamic balance of the yin and yang. The Spiral Dynamics Yellow Integral value system looks to build relationships between the parts, while the Turquoise Holistic eighth value system sees it all as one whole.

In Abram's description of the role of the tribal shaman, we see the kind of work needed to maintain the *"Purple"* integrity of our relationship to life, that has been so lost in industrial civilisation:

> *"By his constant rituals, trances, ecstasies, and 'journeys', he ensures that the relation between human society and the larger society of beings is balanced and reciprocal, and that the village never takes more from the living land that it returns to it–not just materially but with prayers, propitiations, and praise."*[18]

In the previous graphic of Newcomb's, the two first (lowest) energy dynamics (Beige and Purple) are labelled Internal, as are the two last (highest) (Yellow and Turquoise). The central four are labelled External. This points to a basic characteristic difference in those sets of value systems. The internally-focused systems have a more yin based experience of interconnectedness, while the externally-focused systems have a more yang-based experience of distinction.[19]

In the context of our collective human development, our current form of civilisation really emerged at the moment of the split, when the first of the External systems (Red) appeared.[20] We are now reaching a time where a significant percentage of the human population is acceding to the Green value system, the fourth of the External, yang-based systems. (Some people may be surprised to hear the Green system categorised in this way, as it is often labelled as harmony-driven, which it is, but it still essentially focuses on the parts rather than the whole, emphasising diversity, difference, and respect for the individual.) The Cultural Creatives are a good example of the emergence of the Green value system.

The development beyond Green signifies that humanity is now on the verge of re-entering a way of looking at the world with an internal, integrative yin focus (with Yellow integration and Turquoise oneness). This would explain why Grof and others identify so much emergence of yin-based thinking, even though it has not yet matured enough to morph into new forms of organisation and governance structures. This would also explain why Clare Graves, who did the original research behind the Spiral Dynamics model, identified the step from Green to Yellow as being a great leap for humankind.[21]

A key reason why this shift is so important at this time of nonlinear transition and emergence is the need to be able to sense into the subtle patterns of the future that are to be found in the apparent chaos. The yin-based sensing systems are far better equipped to perform that task than the yang-based analytic systems that draw from past knowledge.

Our Volutionary Relationship to Nature

One of the critical reasons why the volution model is important has to do with how people experience and conceptualise their relationship to Nature (in this context I use Nature to mean the physical non-human life on planet Earth). Up until now the developmental models have usually been linear, emphasising a move away from the *"lower"* more embodied levels of development. Dr Matthijs Schouten and Irene van Lippe, in their Living in Relationship course and co-authored book,[22] explore a number of phases that humanity has passed through in our understanding and expression of our relationship to Nature: Ruler, Steward, Partner, Participant, Mystic.

Ruler

The ruler relationship describes a position where humans put ourselves above Nature and see ourselves as needing to dominate and control it. This correlates with the Spiral Dynamics Blue order-driven value system, which emphasises hierarchy and control. The emergence of this value system in itself is critical to our human development (it enables us to find collective agreements on how to live together, for example): as a developmental code, it is a key part of our journey.

However each code can give rise to different content. In this case - particularly in the emerging industrial societies - the content that emerged in relationship to Nature was one of fear of the wild, and a story of our right to dominate and exploit the natural world for our own ends, as emphasised by the Abrahamic religions[23] (which, although they began with a story of dominion and stewardship, ended with a story of domination).[24]

Steward

The steward relationship describes humans as looking after Nature.

Having controlled it in the ruler phase, and now feeling safer around Nature, we start to relate to it more as a child, in a parent-child dynamic. Note that the need to control still lies beneath the surface, but once we have Nature under control, we can *"help it develop"*. This correlates with the emergence of the Orange Achiever-Self value system in Spiral Dynamics. With the underlying drive for continuous progress and growth in this value system code, the emergence of the Industrial Revolution as content within that code became a potent recipe for using Nature to further humanity's ends for ever more comfort and wealth. Nature was tamed and kept in parks and reserves, where we continue to *"steward"* it for our own recreational use.

Partner

The partnership role correlates with Spiral Dynamics' Green Sensitive-Self value system. In this phase, we have had enough of the ongoing strive-drive for more and better. Often it is exhaustion that brings us to the realisation that there is more to life than the illusory rewards of the outside world. We re-connect to our inner worlds, to our emotions, and become aware of the pain and damage we have caused ourselves, each other and the world around us.

At this point we have a strong urge to reconnect to Nature, and start to see ourselves more as equal, yet still apart. As a partner, there is still us and Nature, yet now we do start to see and honour Nature more, and look for possibilities to develop a more conscious relationship to it. We feel how wrong it is to exploit Nature for our own ends and will often raise our voices in protest at exploitative activities and plans.

Participant

The Participant is closest to Spiral Dynamics' Yellow value system. Where the partner still really sees Nature as something to feel sorry for, the Participant starts to realise that there is no choice here: the reality is that humanity is a participant in the broader unfolding of life and we need to start acting accordingly. The Participant understands that all life is connected, and that humanity is a part of the Earth. We seek to participate in the natural processes, to get closer to how life does things. As you will sense from the words above, there is still some distance between the Participant and Nature – we are still seeking to participate in Nature.

Mystic

As Mystic, the boundaries finally fall away and we dissolve into the web of life – yet now we are conscious of that process. There is no ruling over, stewarding of, partnering with or participating in – simply a realisation that we are life and Nature. There is no separation, even though there is differentiation. This stage is far more than simply a cognitive realisation. We feel it in our hearts as we remember who we truly are. Given the trans-cognitive nature of the experience, it is hard to express in words, which is why it is called Mystic, and why mystics tend to be known for expressing themselves in art and poetry more than academic writing. This correlates most closely with the eighth phase in the octave, Spiral Dynamics' Turquoise holistic value system: real communion with Gaia as a living planetary being.

As much as these are civilisational phases of development, each individual also passes through them as we grow up. I certainly recall them all clearly. The shift from Steward to Partner was particularly powerful, with the awakening to Nature as an alive part of my world. Most recently, the transition from Participant to Mystic continues to be a strong experience. The surrender I experience in the realisation of our oneness with all of life is paradigm-shattering. It is particularly strong as it is the first time our development transcends yet includes the cognitive. I feel the grinding of those gears daily!

In this journey, which has included spirals of learning and application, I have come to see the importance of integrating earlier phases of development. From that context, it is surprising that Schouten should leave out three earlier stages of development that are made explicit in the Spiral Dynamics model – Beige survival-driven, Purple safety-driven and Red power-driven. It is important to spend time on these, not so much for the sake of historical accuracy as for the relevance of re-integrating them into our consciousness and lives, for the sake of becoming more whole and able to resonate with all the strings on our fiddle, as it were, and re-engage all of life.[25]

In the Beige system we were one with Nature, a part of Nature, embedded in Nature, unaware of ourselves as separate beings – a pre-cognitive unity state. In the Purple system, we were becoming aware of Nature around us and were still very much communicating with Nature through non-cognitive senses – a natural participation. In the Red system we became aware of our own identity, our power to impact the world around and the power of the world to impact us. We were still in our wild state, connected to the wildness of Nature, but in an increasingly proactive way, where we perceive life as a battle to be the top predator.

The research into volution has lead me to believe that this developmental journey is more than the linear pathway from pre cognitive experience to trans-cognitive experience. One of the key findings has been a relationship between Beige and Turquoise, Purple and Yellow, Red and Green, Orange and Blue, as described above. In the body-based research carried out with Dylan Newcomb (see above), these pairs each ended up having the same basic movements but with a different quality.

The journey then reveals itself to be one of unconscious exploration of life until the mid-point of the journey (between Blue and Orange), and from then on a process of the re-integration of the stages that one has passed through and seemingly left behind. So Orange striving needs to integrate Blue boundaries, Green sensitivity and collectivism needs to integrate Red power and individuation, Yellow interconnecting needs to integrate Purple belonging and Turquoise unity mystical consciousness needs to integrate Beige embodied unity experience, recognising both the wholeness and the individual as a conscious co-creative expression of that whole. The echoes from the earlier partner systems point to what needs to be healed. There is a literal *"re-membering"* as the parts are put back together.

Regress to Progress

"My life is a story of the self-realisation of the unconscious."

CG Jung's opening sentence in the Prologue
to Memories, Dreams, Reflections

*"He knows both knowledge and action, with action overcomes death
and with knowledge reaches immortality.*

*"Into deep darkness fall those who follow the immanent. Into deeper
darkness fall those that follow the transcendent.*

*"One is the outcome of the transcendent, and another is the outcome
of the immanent. Thus have we heard from the ancient sages who
explained this truth to us.*

*"He who knows the transcendent and the immanent, with the immanent
overcomes death and with the transcendence reaches immortality."*

From the Isa Upanishad, in Harvey[26]

As described in the previous section, the integration of earlier phases
is critical to releasing information and energy held in those stages,
so that the later stages can unfold. Wilber elaborates extensively on this
in his book Integral Psychology.[27] Let me turn to my own experience to
illustrate this dynamic.

Over a period of a number of months I experienced a transition in my
own awareness (when I described it to Jude Currivan, she identified
it as the shift into what she called The Eighth Chakra[28] referenced in

her book of the same title,[29] relating to the transition into the eighth Spiral Dynamics Turquoise holistic system. It started with a traumatic experience related to a loss of balance (identified by my doctor as Benign Paroxysmal Positional Vertigo (BPPV)), when all of a sudden the street in front of me tilted to about 45 degrees and I had to run down the hill I suddenly found myself on until I bumped into a wall and the street started to stabilise and return to its original position at 90 degrees to my body.

While my doctor described this as a loose crystal in my ear (BPPV), my therapist wasn't surprised when I told her more about the moment it happened. I was walking along talking to someone I had just had lunch with, and they had said something which had set my mind to thinking about the future implications and actions I would have to take. At that same moment a lorry behind me started to lower its tailgate. The noise of the lorry startled me back to the present moment. I instinctively turned my head towards the noise, and when I turned my head back to face forwards again, the street tilted.

My therapist explained the episode as follows: the work we had been doing over the last year or so had been primarily about my preventing myself from getting so carried away by the thoughts in my head, and becoming more embodied in the present moment. The experience with the lorry provided an extreme example of the polarity I was navigating, the swing between ideas for the future and presence in the moment. The sensitivity of my body to that tension literally knocked me off balance.

The experiences I have had of the fully embodied state she is helping me work towards well match the descriptions of the eighth level of the octave, or the Spiral Dynamics Turquoise value system. This would imply that the earlier level I would be most involved in healing and integrating would be the pre-cognitive body-based Beige survival driven level. That imbalance experience was a shock to my system, and my body clearly perceived it as a life-threatening situation, releasing large amounts of energy in a reptilian brain instinct to fight or flight.

As Peter Levine documents in his book Waking the Tiger: Healing Trauma,[30] if that energy is not released in a successful response to the life-threatening situation in the moment, it remains in the body and creates the symptoms associated with trauma, until it can be decompressed and discharged. It is important to de-link the emotions from the originating event, and fear from arousal, to be able to integrate the original experience. He also notes how a traumatic experience can create a resonance with a previous traumatic experience and trigger the emergence of the energy related to that trauma too.

Following on from the imbalance experience, I lived through ongoing panic and fear attacks - a continual state of high alertness and occasional extreme anxiety symptoms including uncontrollable shaking and tremors in my body. Any pressure from the world around me to perform in any way triggered panic and I was forced to withdraw from most of my daily activities. As I came to understand what was happening, I was able to adopt more of a witness position to my body's responses and avoid getting caught up in the experience, exacerbating it through fear and stressful thoughts of what might be wrong with me.

As I learned to deal with this energy in my body, I discovered ways of transforming the contracted energy into flowing energy. When I feel the anxiety rising again, I bring my awareness to the place in my body where the energy seems to be located, connect to it with acceptance and compassion, greet it, acknowledge the important role it has played in the past, and invite it to reintegrate into my system to help me move forward to the next phase. I literally dive into the tension with my awareness, becoming one with it, at which point it usually starts to move and decompress, spreading out in a tingling feeling throughout my body. I feel relief and joy, and interpret that as being the decompression of a particular traumatised energy.

This experience and Levine's research and findings [31] as a psychologist back up the idea of regression, to heal past traumas and release energy held there, as part of taking a next step forward in our development. For the volution octave to complete its journey from seed to fruit, therefore, the second half of the journey must entail the integration and re-membering of previous stages and healing of past traumas, to allow the emergence of a next phase that is more than the sum of the past parts.

Psychotherapist and shaman Will Taegel [32] emphasises the importance of engaging the *"sub-self"* not only for our individual healing but also to enable us to face our current ecological challenges, getting beyond denial so that we may fully engage ourselves in appropriate responses. In his words, *"Without Nature-based mysticism, non-dual mysticism cannot function, especially in relation to the complex problems of the environmental crisis."* [33]

Richard Gardner frames it this way:

"The evolutionary process will be seen to be the constant integration of the conscious mind with that of the subconscious. A really significant fusion of our dual consciousness will undoubtedly carry with it magical powers and a tremendous increase in understanding."[34]

These subconscious patterns are often held in our body and the integration of the sub-conscious goes hand in hand with the conscious integration of our body, which we split off (as described at the start of this chapter). Aurobindo summarises it beautifully:

"This new relation of the Spirit and the body assumes–and makes possible–free acceptance of the whole of material Nature in place of rejection; the drawing back from her, the refusal of all identification or acceptance, which is the first normal necessity of the spiritual consciousness for its liberation, is no longer imperative. To cease to be identified with the body, to separate oneself from the body consciousness, is a recognised and necessary step whether towards spiritual liberation or towards spiritual perfection and mastery over nature. But this redemption once effected, the descent of the spiritual light and force can invade and take up the body also and there can be a new liberated and sovereign acceptance of material Nature."

Aurobindo, in Harvey[35]

The promise is indeed great but, as I experience it myself, the path is not comfortable. In Shambhavi Chopra's book on Kali, the Hindu goddess of creation and destruction, David Frawley notes in the foreword that

"Purification, which implies the destruction of negativity, must precede any great creation or transformation."[36]

The Human Journey to Wholeness

"The mind shall be God-vision's tabernacle,
The body intuition's instrument,
And life a channel for God's visible power...
The Spirit's tops and Nature's base shall draw
Near to the secret of their separate truth
And know each other as one deity.
The spirit shall look out through Matter's gaze
And Matter shall reveal the Spirit's face.
Then man and superman shall be at one
And all the Earth become a single life."

Aurobindo, from Savitri, in Harvey[37]

As outlined in the section above on our relationship to Nature, it is essential for humanity to discover a sense of conscious reconnection to life around us if we are to successfully navigate the ecological and social challenges that lie ahead. This would reflect the development of the Yellow Integral and Turquoise Holistic stages in the Spiral Dynamics model, and therefore the integration of the Purple connection/ belonging and Beige survival/body/material - as Taegel says, *"return to our roots without losing the brilliance of later developments."*[38]

In the volution model, these are the final steps in the journey from seed to fruit, when a level of integration is achieved that provides the seed for a next major phase. A part of that integration and journey to wholeness for humanity seems to be a capacity for greater awareness of the informational and energetic dimensions of our reality. In Western traditions this is often referred to as psychic abilities, clairvoyance or parapsychology.[39]

In his book Supernormal, Radin documents the academic research providing statistically significant evidence for the existence of psychic phenomena. In Where Science and Magic Meet, Roney-Dougal also reviews the research and offers an integrative framework for understanding the different phenomena that have been observed. Importantly to our point here, she also observes:

"Most esoteric traditions and recent experimentation in parapsychology share this concept: that greater awareness of the subconscious, and an ability to control its functioning more, will eventually enable us to live at a level of mind in which we can utilise our psi abilities with some form of conscious control."[40]

Once more we see how the integration of earlier stages of development and past events is linked to the release of more advanced abilities to access a more interconnected reality. In human development as seen through the lens of Spiral Dynamics, Beige and Purple are pre-cognitive stages of development, and so our experiences in those phases of our lives are held primarily in the subconscious. This is precisely what Roney-Dougal says we must engage with if we are to achieve conscious control of our psi abilities, which would naturally emerge through the Yellow-Integral and Turquoise-Holistic phases. Currivan also documents research that *"suggests that the conscious mind of the ego-self generally filters out nonlocal psi perceptions from its ordinary awareness."*[41] In other words, to access these perceptions we need to be able to consciously interact with the subconscious.

In my experience of dowsing and energetic work, and in the research and teaching of Hans Andeweg,[42] we access the energetic information through the body. We must reconnect to the denser aspect of our being in order to develop its more subtle informational aspects, much as a tree must grow deeper roots to put forth higher branches. Many people have also documented how important it is to work with the body when trying to heal trauma held in the subconscious.[43] This is explained well by the volution model as outlined above.

Why, one might ask, has life created this process of incarnating into a relative world with its seemingly linear journey full of pain and trauma, only to require us to reintegrate and heal it all again later? In essence, this process enables life to learn consciously. As described above, the process of informational entropy creates the linear reality of time.[44] As Currivan notes, *"these intrinsic conditions of causality not only enable the Universe to unfold and evolve but allow the level of human consciousness associated with the ego-self to experience the implications of making choices through the process of cause and effect and thereby accrue learning."*[45] For life to learn, it needs to be able to make choices which make an impact that life can learn from and improve on. That has to happen in a linear, relative reality.

The Individual Experience of Time

As outlined in the descriptions above, there are phases in the volutionary journey from seed to fruit. However they are not as linear as developmental psychology has generally described them to date.

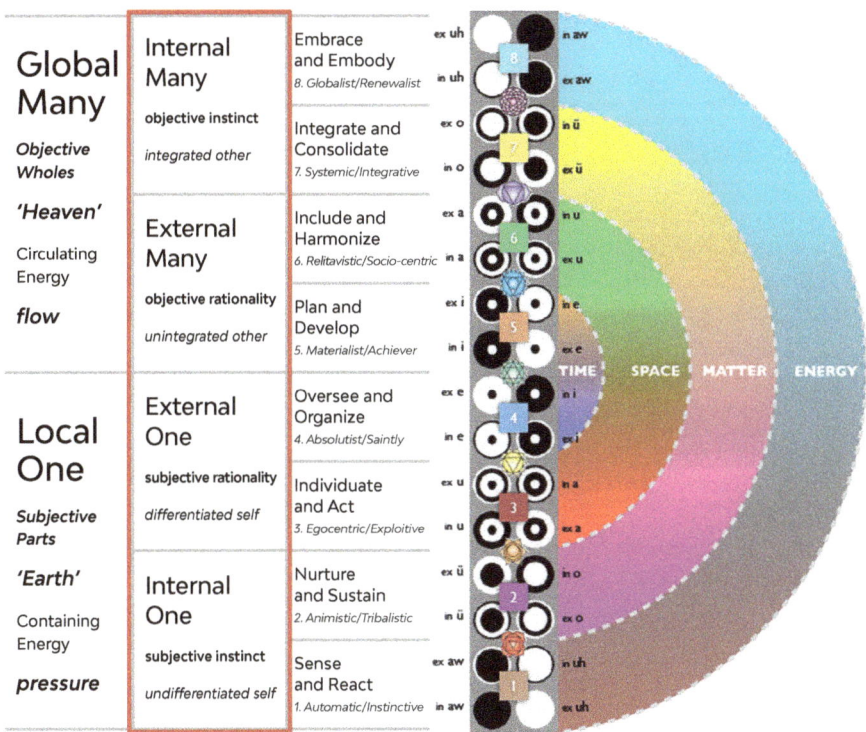

Figure 35 : *The Yin-Yang Dynamic at the level of Four Phases*

It is possible to look through the lens of the four volutionary phases and, for example, through the lens of Spiral Dynamics, which is one expression of the underlying volutionary dynamics. Referring back to Figure 35, we can start to explore how the phases unfolding in us as individuals impact how we see and experience life and the voluntionary process. The descriptions in the red box point to similarities between the top and bottom sections - both are internally-focused and neither are differentiated (*"undifferentiated"* and *"integrated"*).

One of the major struggles of physics in recent decades has been explaining how things sometimes seem to show up as particles and sometimes as waves (as in the double-slit experiment). The difference seems to lie in whether something has been observed or not.

If it has been observed as a result, then it shows up with the characteristics of a particle. If it has been observed not as a result but as a process, it shows up with the characteristics of a wave.[46] The volution model ties in nicely with this experience.

A wave is an interconnected movement, as opposed to a separate, differentiated object, like a particle. The volution model proposes that the wave-like experience of reality dominates in the two lower and the two higher notes in the Spiral Dynamics octave, whereas the particle-like experience of reality dominates in the four central value systems.*

In the volution model described above, the torus is breathing in and out, from less formed and less differentiated reality on the expansive, in-breath exterior of the torus, to more formed and more differentiated and crystallised reality in the contractive, out-breath interior of the torus.

---

* Although I talk here about a particle-like and wave-like experience of reality, what is experienced as a particle is more likely to be not a collapse of the wave as quantum physicists originally described it but more the cohering of a wave function through the act of observation.[47]

In the lower outer value systems of the Spiral Dynamics model, Beige and Purple, the experience of reality is primarily a pre-rational one of an interconnected world, where the relationships between the parts dominate. In the upper outer value systems, Yellow and Turquoise, the experience is also one of increasing interconnectedness and interdependence, yet this time from a post-cognitive awareness that is conscious of earlier phases and can see their relationships to each other.

In the lower central value systems, Red and Blue, the focus has shifted to separation and distinction - Red with the emergence of the ego-self and awareness of oneself as separate from the world around, and Blue bringing that into the collective awareness by creating hierarchical distinctions between people and separating things into systems and structures. In the upper central value systems, Orange and Green, people engage with the differentiated more consciously. Orange enjoys playing all the different parts off against each other in a game to gain as much as possible. Green thrives on seeing the uniqueness of each individual and celebrating that diversity. In the outer systems therefore the priority is more on wave-like relationships of the whole and in the central systems more on the particle-like distinctions of the parts.

Time is also experienced differently. In the central systems, things seems to move fast as our attention is drawn to the externally manifest parts zooming around. We experience more the flow of information within space-time as entropy.[48] In the outer systems, we are more present in the moment (consciously in the later stages and unconsciously in the earlier ones) and things slow down, as the relational space shifts to the foreground of our awareness with the busyness of the parts moving to the background.

We experience information more non-locally. The central four value systems also exhibit thinking that is much more about certainty, knowing and a fixed understanding of reality. Conversely, the outer four value systems exhibit thinking that is more about uncertainty and not-knowing (inducing fear in the lower two and wonder and curiosity in the upper two). This makes sense if we see the first two stages as an entering phase of a new expression of life, where the system isn't firmed up yet in its identity, and the last two stages as an exiting phase of the system, where it is beginning to blur the boundaries of its identity as it starts to see itself as connected to a bigger whole and preparing to move on to its next incarnation. The central stages are where the self really crystallises its form in this current manifestation. Both the particle-like and wave-like aspects of reality are always present, but our experience of them changes depending on which volutionary phase we are in.

This implies that the more differentiated thinking of the central four systems co-arises with an experience of reality more as being composed of particle-like separate parts. This perception informs the kinds of decisions we make about how to engage with the world around us. It has the advantage of enabling life to see itself in all its uniqueness and diversity, yet starts to create problems when it forgets the inherent interconnectedness underlying the diversity.

That is a make-or-break moment for a system: can it re-member its wholeness in time to reconnect its parts and complete its octave journey, thereby fulfilling its potential as a mature fruit-ion of its initial seed-potential impulse? Or will it tear itself apart by pushing the differentiation to such extremes that it destroys the relational tissue that holds it all together?

I suggest that this is where humanity finds itself at this time, and why this dissertation is being written through me as an expression of humanity, in a quest to reconnect the parts. It would also be why Currivan writes *"All matter, which we consider to be solid, is thus essentially wave-like and energetic"*[49] and why this perception is growing amongst humanity: we are moving into the final two phases of the octave and starting to consciously perceive the interconnected nature of reality, whilst also acknowledging that the particle-like reality, too, exists - not exclusively particle-like, as the central four systems perceive it, but as an expression of reality that plays out in a greater interconnected whole.

Another dynamic of the linear aspect of this process is that as a system unfolds, it becomes increasingly aware of itself and all its parts. In the human story, as our awareness develops to be able to apprehend ever more of reality, we see and simultaneously co-create increasing differentiation in life. At the same time as we expand our knowledge of space and the Universe on a large scale around us, we become increasingly aware of the parts of life at the smallest scales. This same dynamic holds up both at the level of our cognitive understanding and at the emotional level. As our self-awareness expands, so we are able to reach down into the deeper regions of ourselves to transform trauma and blocked energy held from the past.

Another way to express this is that at any one moment, a wave-like perspective describes the relational space, while a particle-like perspective describes the material aspects. These are two perspectives on the same moment. As they grow closer and become more integrated, the consciousness of the entity is able to perceive more of both. They are two poles of one spectrum breathing in and out.

This thesis does not imply that the particle-like differentiation suddenly diminishes as we move into the more wave-like relational awareness of the later phases. On the contrary, our more expanded wave-like awareness can hold more of reality without getting fixated on specific parts, and in doing so can observe more of life. In this observing we can identify more of the parts (observation is what creates the particle-like characteristics of something) and engage consciously with them. From this perspective, although a wave-like or particle-like awareness dominates in different phases, both the volume of the interconnected wave and the diversity of the unique particles continue to increase on a system's volutionary journey from seed to fruit.

At the same time, the later phases display an ability to hold a wave-like perspective capable of suspending knowing and judgement, thereby releasing our experience from fixity in its current form, to transform more rapidly in relationship with everything around it, in a way that is beneficial for the whole. The wave-particle distinction thus starts to converge as the characteristics of fixed matter become increasingly malleable and the probabilities and possibilities of wave-like reality become increasingly able to manifest in form.

This is a final integration of relative diversity and absolute connectedness in non-duality. It is the integration of Currivan's First Law of Information, where information is expressed as energy-matter and universally conserved (as in Quantum Theory), and her Second Law of Information, where information is expressed entropically as space-time where space expands and time flows (as in Relativity Theory)[50] Currivan summarises in this way: *"The first Law enables our Universe to exist, the second to evolve."*[51]

Neuroscience and Eco-fields

"As above, so below, as within, so without, as the Universe, so the soul."
Hermes Trismegistus, Copenhaver[52]

During a course on Neuroscience and Eco-fields,[53] and through my own experience over the duration of that course, I gained clarity on a thesis I will expand on in this section, which reinforces the view on the volutionary holographic nature of reality. My thesis is that, as people shift their interior experience and patterns, so the world around us changes. The reverse is equally true: as people create change in the information fields of the world around them, so that is reflected in changes in our interior experience and nervous system. This is the reason for connecting neuroscience and eco-fields, and selecting the Hermes Trismegistus *"as within, so without"* quote above. The two main faculty members of the course also reflect these two aspects – Jim Hickman on neuroscience and Will Taegel on eco-fields.

Self-Directed Neuroplasticity

During the course, Hickman and Stanley Krippner repeatedly pointed out that there is now significant scientific evidence demonstrating that we human beings can alter our own nervous system. This can be achieved through practices of inner awareness and consciously directed intention. Hickman referred to Stephen Hawking's term *"model-dependent realism"*[54] which describes how the models in our brains shape our experience of reality. These models can both limit us to our existing patterns and ways of experiencing the world around us, and be re-scripted as we take more conscious responsibility for how we experience and therefore engage and contribute to that world.

Hickman referenced research showing how spiritual and religious practices can positively impact our brain and nervous system.[55] He also noted how many of the patterns that deeply influence people's interaction with life are rooted in layers of the brain that developed early on, before the emergence of the cognitive and self-reflective layers and abilities. This implies that we cannot access those layers purely through the cognitive mind, but need to address them through more emotional and somatic interventions, as described in previous sections. This has been demonstrated, for example, by the comprehensive work of Stanislav Grof with his holotropic breathwork practices and research.[56]

During this course, I was processing some trauma from my childhood that had risen to the surface at that time. On the one hand, I was working with a therapist who was helping me become more aware of some of the dynamics at play, enabling me to see them and name them, bringing the light of my awareness into some of the darker shadows, converting those patterns from *"subject"* (where they are so much part of me that I can't see them) to *"object"*, where I can consciously choose whether to associate with them or not. On the other hand, I was taking these traumas and their implications into a breathing practice I had been doing for a number of years, that had always proven powerful in transforming limiting beliefs and patterns that no longer serve me (the practice is called Quantum Light Breath, developed by Jeru Kabbal.[57] I would like to focus on this breathing practice for a moment.

As stated above, neuroscience shows us that foundational patterns in how we engage the world are located in pre-cognitive layers of our brain. To access and transform them, we need to engage in more somatic practices. This has been my experience with the breathing practice. The process normally lasts about an hour. The basic instruction is to develop a deep breathing that fills both the lower and upper lungs fully, and then release it. You start slowly, getting used to the full breathing, then increase the pace, then go through a few minutes of breathing as fully and fast as possible, then relax the breath again and slow it down as you come to the end – always maintaining the full breath.

Biologically, you are pumping more oxygen into your system than it is used to, more than it needs for normal operation, providing an excess to feed other processes that you can direct with your intention. The breathing process is accompanied by instructions from Kabbal. In essence, he continually brings your awareness back to the breath, allowing other thoughts and emotions to be there, but not directing your attention to them. At the outset, he asks you identify the issue (belief, emotion, quality) you want to transform, and imagine it written on a sticky label and stuck on your body at the place of your choosing. After the first warm-up period of about 20 minutes, he then reminds you of the issue that you identified at the beginning and invites any early memories to come to the surface that may be related to that issue. At the same time he asks you to increase the pace of your breathing, culminating in an intense few minutes of maximum speed (whist maintaining the fullness of the breath).

At the end of the intense period, he slows the breath down again and invites you to see the sticker with your issue on it come loose from your body, fall off your body, shrink and disappear (I visualise it disappearing down my grounding cord to the centre of the Earth). The instructions then focus on allowing the light and love in, connecting to your heart, to the centre of your joy, and to remembering who you truly are.

This process has always been a powerful experience for me. It is a very physical and emotional experience. I usually shout at some points, sometimes with anger and frustration, sometimes with joy, sometimes in defiance. In these sessions I have sobbed like never before and laughed hysterically. My body always responds physically, with energy flowing to different parts of my body, with me often kicking or stamping my feet, and banging my fists on the floor (I do it lying down).

Sometimes clear memories arise of moments from earlier in my life, other times I just get raw emotion and energy in my body. Letting go of the sticky label is without exception a massive release that brings relief, joy and love flooding into my system. I usually come out of these processes feeling completely different than when I started an hour earlier – grounded, with extreme clarity and in authentic compassionate relationship with those around me. In my journal, following one breathing session, I wrote:

"In QLB today I took in the feeling of being disconnected and isolated - from primarily the feelings in myself and in others, but also the simple feeling of being alone as I had at school. Again, tears and sobbing at the release. Ultimate insight was that it was all about love - love is connection. Accepting the love for myself, my partner, the kids, the Earth and all life."

I share the example of the breathing practice because, for me, it backs up the claims of self-directed neuroplasticity. There is no doubt in my mind, from my direct experience, that I can shift limiting patterns and beliefs in my system that would otherwise have remained hidden to me, and both experience and co-create a different world around me as a result. I also share it because the very physical experience I have in this breathing process also occurs, though with less force, when I am working energetically with a system 'outside' myself – such as an organisation or relationship.

In the following section I will explore my experience of interacting energetically with *"eco-fields"* and the correlation with our neuroplasticity.

Eco-fields

In Wild Heart, Dr Taegel describes what he calls an eco-field:

> *"I define an eco-field as that region of influence which underlies a given ecology, a specific locale. The various eco-fields emerge out of a more profound field, itself emergent from the Primordial Mind. Within the specific environment, energy exchanges occur in such a manner as to encourage the resilience and evolution of the intertwined parts making up the greater whole."*[58]

Hans Andeweg[59] describes natural systems in a similar way, and then goes one step further to extend the concept of an eco-field to other entities such as organisations and projects. In her work on co-creative science, Machaelle Small Wright[60] also expanded her work with energy in gardens to apply the same principles and practices to what she calls *"soil-less gardens"*.

It is my belief that anything with a name and a boundary has an energetic field in which *"exchanges occur in such a manner as to encourage the resilience and evolution of the intertwined parts making up the greater whole"*, as Taegel describes. Even with a more abstract project that has no specific permanent physical and geographic location, all different levels of energetic entity are participating, such as angels, devas and nature spirits.[61]

I have continued my energetic work with organisations and systems, and with Ubiquity University in particular, applying the practices I learned with Andeweg in the ECOintention training along with the self taught Perelandra work. I have started to notice and be curious about how my body reacts when I am carrying out an informational energetic intervention. I will take the Perelandra work as an example.

In the Perelandra co-creative process, you set up a 'coning' with different energetic entities – the deva of the project you are working on, Pan and the nature spirits, the angelic realm and your own higher Self.[62] Every so often, in my case usually weekly, you call a meeting in the coning with your energetic partners, give an update on recent developments, frame your goals for the coming period, and ask if any intervention is needed to help the system achieve those goals. You dowse a list of possible interventions for relevance.

Once you have identified what needs doing, you then carry out the intervention. It usually includes the use of some kind of essence, which is liquid imprinted with information. You then administer a certain number of drops of the essence by putting them on a spoon and asking the essence of the drops to be shifted to the project – during which the information contained in the essence is transferred to the energetic architecture of the project.[63] During this ten-second process, when the information is apparently being transferred from the essence of the liquid in the spoon to the information field of the organisation, I get a physical reaction. My body always responds in some way, most often with movement in the skin around my scalp, and with a sense of high voltage interactions in my brain – literally as if it is being rewired. My spine normally also tenses in different ways. After a while my body relaxes again, which I take as a sign that the information transfer has been completed.

The question which arises for me is: *"Why should my body physically respond in this way when I am transferring one thing outside me to something else outside me?"* If we consider the hermetic statement *"as within, so without"* and many other teachings emphasising that our inner and outer worlds are reflections of each other, then it is not so surprising. The implication is that the informational and energetic changes created by my intervention in the systems I am working with are reflected within my own body and nervous system.

While this statement may be easy to accept conceptually, when I actually experience it and contemplate that experience, it really does challenge the way I, and most people, assume the world works (through cause-and-effect interactions of separate parts). For me, although I have not yet done enough research to scientifically validate this thesis, it points to a realisation that the informational changes I make in the world I perceive around me are mirrored in informational changes within my own system. This is where neuroscience and eco-field science start to engage each other. Dr. Taegel, in the early stages of the course, pointed to how the human brain and the Earth's system mirrored each other. He also described how microtubules in our cells link us to informational fields in the world around us. All this points to a growing realisation of the unity of interior and exterior that Hermes pointed to all those years ago.

As Within, So Without

"Humanity emulates Earth,
Earth emulates heaven,
heaven emulates the Way,
the Way emulates Nature."

Lao Tzu from the Tao Te Ching, in Harvey[64]

"Just as the wounder wounds himself, so the healer heals himself."

CG Jung[65]

"I noticed when I came back from my therapist the other day and was completely connected with my caring loving energy, how immediately the world around me responded. Marcella (my wife) was caring and relaxed, as were the boys. It really is true that our inner state is reflected in the world around us. I felt it even in the moment as more recently I shifted my energy as we interacted and Marcella's energy changed with me." Journal Entry[66]

My experiential learning in this domain of inner and outer interconnectedness and mutual plasticity has mostly taken place in the field of my closest relationships, namely with my wife and my three sons. The journal entry above describes an experience that significantly helped to embed this perspective in my view of the world. I suddenly became acutely aware of how the world around me literally responded as I shifted my inner state. It wasn't a cause-effect type of experience, as there was no lag time. It was simultaneous, as if it were one thing. There was a moment of deep shock as I saw myself shifting my irritation into care and in the same moment my wife literally became a different person before my eyes: from an expression of stress and repressed anger to openness and connection. Since then I have practiced this shift in different contexts, and my experience bears it out each time. On our fridge, we now have a quote from Wayne Dyer: *"If you change the way you look at things, the things you look at change."*

Such informational and energetic interaction seems to take place in a nonlinear dimension of reality, as the shifts happen instantaneously. This would reflect Currivan's First Law of Information.[67] Krippner described dreams as being in a similar dimension, relating this to chaos theory. Twenty-eight years of research at Princeton University's engineering department[68] demonstrated that human intention does indeed impact what would otherwise be random events in the material world – and that such interactions can happen outside of the linear parameters of time and space.

While work is still ongoing in this regard[69] there is dwindling doubt as to the interconnection between neuroplasticity and the human capacity to impact the informational eco-fields in the world we experience around us – whether from a Princetonian scientific perspective or from my own personal experience. As Currivan[70] points out, the research demonstrates that the way information is observed is critical to how that information takes form as energy and matter.

"The progressive understanding... of how information underlies and pervades its appearance is crucial to real-ising how the environment and observer are integrally interconnected with any and all experiments. In other words there's no separate 'objective' reality and the entirety of our Universe is an integrated, coherent and in-formational entity."

Abram postulates that the development of the idea of an *"inner world"* interior to the human being and residing in our minds and psychology is part of the problem. That inner dimension of reality exists in all life, as part of everything in us and around us. The split between our inner world and the world around us is due to *"the loss of our ancestral reciprocity with the animate Earth"*.

"When the elemental powers that surround us are suddenly construed as having less significance than ourselves, when the generative Earth is abruptly defined as a determinate object devoid of its own sensations and feelings, then the sense of our wild and multiplicitous otherness must migrate, either into a supersensory heaven beyond the natural world, or else into the human skull itself – the only allowable refuge, in this world, for what is ineffable and unfathomable."[71]

CG Jung goes as far to say *"knowledge does not enrich us; it removes us more and more from the mythical world in which we were once at home by right of birth."*[72]

The quality of inner experience actually permeates all life. We have just stopped seeing and experiencing the world in that way. Talbot describes the Sufi experience of *"an inner world that 'turns out to envelop, surround, or contain that which at first was out and visible.'"*[73] That sounds a lot like the brane of a torus!

Cultural Volution

One of the initial triggers for my research was a quest to understand how it could be that so many ancient civilisations seem to have been able to achieve remarkable feats of architecture and technology, many of which we are only now realising have resonance with recent findings of science. Anne Baring's description of the phases of cultural development[74] - Lunar, Solar, Integration - provide some explanation for this, as does the octave perspective in the volution model that identifies the final two stages as re-integrating the yin energy that was present in the first two phases. The fact that the yin/Lunar perspective reflects more a wave-like experience of reality (as compared to a yang/ Solar particle-like experience) could explain why we are now (re-) discovering some of the ancient civilisations and their technologies, and noticing their resonance with our latest scientific discoveries and spiritual insights.

Currivan, for example, describes how the Egyptians and Chaldeans *"perceived the relationships within and between numbers and geometry as resonant wave-guides, archetypal pathways for energetic forms and structures to manifest."*[75] Schneider likewise illustrates how numbers and patterns show up across nature, art and science.[76] Drunvalo Melchizedek describes archeological findings of ancient inscriptions on walls of the *"Flower of Life"* symbol, which has embedded within it the fundamental designs of life.[77]

Researchers have confirmed, moreover, that nowadays we would be able to engrave the symbols in that way only using advanced laser technologies. Much has also been written on the technologically advanced nature of the Mayan civilisations, the practices of their shamans and how these seem increasingly relevant to our times.[78] Jahn and Dunne describe their discoveries at six ancient sites in the UK where they *"measured the frequencies of the acoustic standing waves"*. They found:

> *"that the resonant frequencies in all of them were well-defined, lying within the narrow interval between 95 and 120Hz, well within the range of the adult male voice. Even more surprising was the observation that the extensive rock art at some of the locations displayed striking similarities to the standing wave patterns that characterised these chambers."*[79]

They concluded that *"the structures themselves had been built with a deliberate intent to produce specific acoustical resonances, and that their builders had sophisticated understanding of the nature of sound."*[80] Further research into the effects of frequencies on brain activity lead them also to suggest *"that these structures may have played a role in generating altered-state ritual-driven experiences."*[81] As science started to emerge from the pre-rational stages of development, a powerful combination of the experiential sensory and analytical occurred. Jahn and Dunne observed:

"The early scientific heritage that evolved through the cultures of the Egyptians, Greeks, Romans, Orientals, Byzantines, and Medieval alchemists involved intimate admixtures of metaphysical rituals with rigorous analytical techniques, yet they generated extensive pragmatic knowledge and products, some of which, like the ancient pyramids or stone circles, still defied modern replication or full comprehension." [82]

No one has adequately explained how the Egyptian pyramids or the great stone circles were built, with their astronomical alignment and sound qualities. [83] In a similar vein, we have the story of the crystal skulls, [84] broadcast as a documentary on BBC1 and many other channels worldwide. It describes skulls seemingly sculpted from a single piece of crystal, yet scientists at computer company Hewlett Packard acknowledged they could find no trace of tool marks.

Not only do these skulls play an important role in a number of the stories of native people on the American continent, but modern-day psychics have found them to have psi-related qualities. Then there is the great enigma of Atlantis, over which much has been written by both archaeologists and intuitives [85]: a civilisation with apparently highly advanced technology and consciousness that was ultimately unable to channel it constructively and so disappeared under the ocean. Van Daniken, [86] too, has suggested that there is more to ancient discoveries than a solely archaeological interest. Leviton [87] has documented how mythological stories about places contain information on the energetic features of those places. There is of course much controversy about all these phenomena, with a mix of new-age fantasy and scientific-rational close-mindedness confusing the work of authentic intuitives and open-minded scientific researchers.

Either way, the volution model provides a theoretical explanation for why ancient civilisations might have seemed to have access to technologies we are only just discovering with our advanced science: namely that we are actually re-discovering them in the context of the integration of our original wave-based consciousness with the particle based consciousness that has so dominated our perspectives over the last couple of thousand years.

Another clue to the voluntary experience of people living in more of a tribal, pre-rational world, can be found in the use of the word *"wyrd"* by the Anglo-Saxons, Celts and Vikings of north-western Europe. *"Wyrd"* referred to the interconnected web that generates all life and came to be linked with the concept of fate. It was the place the magicians went to in order to help heal people and sense into the emerging future. Wyrd only came to be *"weird"* meaning strange or different after the split. *"Wyrd"* stems from the indo-european stem *"wert-"* which means to spin, turn or rotate. [88]

Once more a sign of the spinning voluntary torus. *"Wyrd"* transformed into *"werden"* in German which means to become. We have the spinning web that generates life - sounds like our torus to me!" [89]

With space-time an entropic expression of information, [90] we can imagine that the wavelengths and frequencies of the integration phase we are currently in resonate with the earlier lunar phase in a way that the solar phase did not, and that this is why we are having related insights.

This collective reintegration, where we seem to be revisiting our cultural past, reflects the process described above for individuals, where we revisit earlier stages of development to release energy blocked there, making that energy available to complete our current octave journey. This collective turn demonstrates the holographic and fractal nature of volution, the dynamics of which can be seen within the Spiral Dynamics model. The alternation of *"express-self"* (yang) and *"sacrifice-self"* (yin) driven value systems has been described with reference to individuals.

These dynamics also show up in the collective field, where they may be recognised not only in terms of *"express-self"* and *"sacrifice-self"*, but also in terms of eras of greater chaos and eras of greater order. The *"express-self"* energy tends to generate more dynamism and chaos, whereas the sacrifice-self energy tends to generate more order and structure.

The Purple tribal era was about bonding and connection within the tribe, contrasted with the Red feudal era which was a period of warlords and winner-takes-all. The ensuing Blue One-Truth-based era saw the emergence of an order born from people buying into a religious (literally *"to bind"*) belief system and strictly following its edicts. Swinging back the other way, the Orange achievement-driven scientific-rational era emerged, where people were encouraged to question everything, find their own way, and be the best individual they could.

This move has created the increasing stress and malaise we now experience in Western societies at the individual level, as well as the chaos we are experiencing ecologically and culturally as our life support systems start to deteriorate, conflict grows and peoples start to migrate in large numbers to find safer places to live.

The Green harmony-driven era again seeks to create more order by connecting everyone up as one big happy family. As the integrative Yellow Integral and Turquoise Holistic value systems emerge, with Turquoise completing the octave shift to the transpersonal, the Internet can perhaps be seen as an external representation of the expansion of our own collective informational membrane that will embrace the planet and beyond.

In his treatment of the Mayan calendar, Calleman[91] likewise illustrates the fractal nature of time and the swings between yin (*"nights"*) and yang (*"days"*).

The most fundamental fractal polarity dynamics of life therefore - the yin and the yang - play out at both individual and collective levels, and always within the context of an underlying unity, as the yin-yang symbol so well illustrates with the seed of the one pole always present in the other. The wave at the centre of the yin-yang symbol represents the integration and third creative dynamic. We have seen that some of the ancient civilisations explicitly practice holding these two forces in a dynamic balance.

The Egyptian priests, for example, saw how *"the manifest world arose from the sundering of cosmic Unity,"* which is why they used bonding rituals to demonstrate the integration of Horus' cosmic unifying power with the physical pharaoh who ruled in the relative world.[92]

Organisational Volution

Volutionary dynamics can also be seen playing out in organisations as a particular form of the collective. This section will explore the theme of the leader-community tension as a collective moves into and through transition.

Transition

It is important first to frame what I mean by 'transition'. There are many different kinds of change, from a small upgrade to the current reality, through a quest into the past or possible futures, to a full-scale change of a system to something different.[93] With the term 'transition', I am talking about the latter, often referred to as a non-linear change, *"macroshift"* or process of emergence.[94]

A number of characteristics define this kind of change. Firstly, all parts of any system are involved in the change. It is not just one element, but literally a whole-system change. Secondly, from the standpoint of the old reality, one cannot see what the system is going to become. The nature of the change is so significant that, when we are immersed in the current or old ways of thinking and doing, we do not have the space to conceive of how different the new system will be. Thirdly, it is an emergent process of change. That means that the change is birthed by the system itself, stimulated by the life conditions it is embedded in, so that the whole system metamorphoses into something completely new. In this process, it is impossible to predict exactly when the change will happen, and one cannot control and design the change process. One can only seek to put in place the most favourable conditions for the system to go through its own process of transformation. This combination of conditions makes this kind of emergent change unlike any other.

The Energy of Transitions

How can we understand such transitions in terms of energy?

This kind of non-linear transition is measurable energetically. In the ECOintention practice[95] that I studied for four years, there are two main types of project descriptors. One type is for projects that - in the initial energetic scan - identify themselves as wanting to achieve their maximum effectiveness and efficiency in their current form, and the other is for projects identifying as wanting to transform into something different.

Over the 20 years of ECOintention practice, the number of projects wanting to optimise their current form has dwindled, while the number wanting to transform into something else has increased to the extent that now it is very rare to find a project of the first sort. That would fit with the understanding that our planet is currently in a macroshift[96] involving all life on Earth. Leading this kind of change as the energetic steward requires certain qualities and competencies that I will explore later.

What all of these theories and practices point to is that entities at all levels have their own wholeness and agency, represented by their *"eco-field"* or energetic architecture. That field displays intelligence in that it interacts with information from within its boundaries and from its environment, and works to optimise resilience and coherence for the system as a whole. It is possible to contact this field and interact with it through our consciousness and intention, as Andeweg, Taegel and Small Wright all affirm.

During a course on this topic, as we explored the relationship between an individual leader and the collective of people they lead, the image of the torus came to me as it related to the energetic architecture.

The torus arises in a tension field between two poles. The axis runs right through the centre of the torus and can be seen as the black hole at the core. In a holographic understanding of reality, the event horizon of the black hole is where all the information is stored.[97] At that centre is a fundamental polarity that creates a pull on the unified field to create relative form.[98]

Once the one is divided, relativity and distinguished forms emerge, in a journey of ongoing refinement, the fundamentals of which are described in the I Ching as it progresses from 1 to 2 to 4 to 8 to 16 and so on, continually refining the original yin-yang tension. Indeed at its foundational level at the core of the Universe, information is expressed as digitised bits in binary quantisation within energy-matter.[99] The nature of the polarity at the centre of the torus, and therefore at the centre of the *"eco-field"* or energetic architecture of all life, is a yin-yang tension, clothed in the specific nature of each individual entity. That yin-yang tension pulls on the unified field, creating a spin dynamic forming the flow shape of a torus and holding within it all platonic solids that underpin all matter.[100] This is the fundamental architecture of anything that can be distinguished out of the unified field, as described in an earlier chapter.

There are a number of different ways to name the yin-yang tension. Small Wright[101] describes creation as happening in the dynamic between involution and evolution. Evolution is the yang-like expansive force that looks to the future and puts out vision and intention. Involution is the yin-like gravitational force that grounds things and pulls them into form and energy-matter in the manifested present. This tension is responsible for the process of creation, which I name *"volution"*.

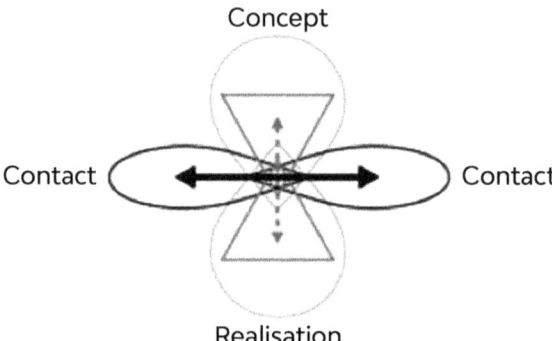

Figure 36 : *ECOintention Levels*   (Andeweg 2016)

Andeweg[102] describes the same creative tension process in terms of three levels: a concept level, which is the more evolutionary pole where plans are made (corresponding, I believe, with what Small Wright refers to as *"Mental Level Activity"*), a realisation level, which is the involutionary dimension manifest in matter (what Small Wright calls the *"Project Framework"*) and a middle - or communication or contact - level arising at a ninety degree plane in between the other two poles.* This latter level is the dimension where information is exchanged within the entity itself and with its environment (Small Wright does not refer to a third level in between).

---

* Currivan[103] provides more evidence for the importance of the ninety degree plane from physics: *"the most important reason for 3-D is the nature of the electro-magnetic field. Pervading space it too requires precisely three orthogonal dimensions to behave in the way it does. The electric and magnetic components of the field are at right angles to each other, with the consequential E-M radiation being at right angles to both."* She also refers to esoteric teachings that describe squares and square roots of numbers as *"dimensional shifts"*.

In Andeweg's work, the middle level emerges as a result of the integration of the other two. He himself says this is a toroidal dynamic.[104] Integration is when the system reaches maturity, meaning that it has been able to transform the concept or intention into manifestation, operating with great coherence, efficiency and adaptability, in a flow state.

Figure 37 : *ECOintention Integration* (Andeweg 2016)

This is represented in this image (Figure 37) of the interlocking triangles, depicting the situation where the mature system has achieved a steady dynamic balance, with ideas and action coherently aligned.

It is in the nature of life, however, to want to evolve towards ever greater wholeness and differentiation at the same time (this could also be framed as greater complexity and awareness). In this regard a stable system is likely to be ready to shift again in the future.[105]

The impulse for that shift is likely to have its roots in two sources: a build-up of excess creative energy within the system itself due to the routine nature of its current stability, and/or the awareness of changes in its operating reality/environment.

At that point, a leader playing their role of energetic steward well, is likely to pick up those signals and start looking for what is next for the system. Many people operating within the system may not yet be aware of the emerging impulse, due to their focus on running the current version well. This is where tension arises between leadership and community.

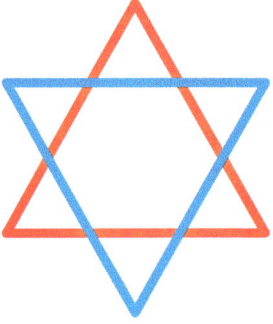

Figure 38 : *ECOintention Transformation* (Andeweg 2016)

What the system wants to do next can be represented by the triangles pushing through each other, as in Figure 38. This symbol is common in many traditions as a representation of transformation (e.g. the star of David, or star tetrahedron in three dimensions).

The process is often turbulent, as the system has to push through a point of great resistance where it has locked into its stable form. That movement creates the start of a new spiral of integration of concept and realisation.

A new idea has emerged, and the system must work out how to turn that idea or vision into reality. This also causes the middle contact level to contract for a while, as communication internally and externally becomes less clear while people work out what this vision and new step really means, what the system needs to count on people for to deliver the new vision, what roles need to be played and which people can best play those roles.

Leadership and Community

In this kind of context, where a leader or leadership team can see the change that is coming before most others in the system, due to their role and their particular qualities, a tension arises between what leadership feels needs to happen, what other people in the organisation can see and the daily activity that still needs to take place to keep the current system running.

If we refer back to the toroidal model, we can see the leadership role at this point as focusing primarily on the vertical axis – the axis that connects present and future. The leadership has just stretched that vertical axis to a bigger vision, as in the expanded image of the interlocking triangles (Figure 39).

Figure 39 : *ECOintention Expansion* (Andeweg 2016)

The tension field within which the organisation is to manifest its work has been increased. The manifestation happens at the ninety degree horizontal plane emanating out from the centre of the torus, like Andeweg's middle level. You can see this process happening in galaxies, for example (Figure 40).

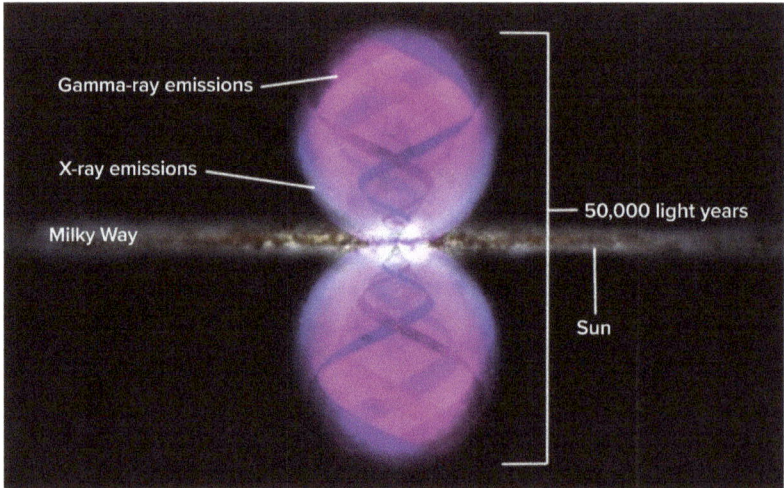

Figure 40 : *Galactic Torus with Manifestation at Ninety Degree Plane*

Most people in the system are focused on this horizontal plane, turning the vision into form. As the vertical tension field intensifies, it puts pressure on the horizontal manifestation plane to expand and adapt too. Yet that can only happen as the vision starts to ground and the system works out the implications in new principles, practices and structures.

The challenge facing the leader is to hold the expanded vision, invite others in the system to join in working out what needs to be done to manifest that vision, all the while honouring the work that has been done so far, much of which will still need to continue to be done, as the past represents the foundation on which the future vision must build.

This kind of transition is so challenging for the people involved because not only will the system have to change, but the people will have to transform as well – or eventually leave the organisation. This personal transformation will necessarily entail healing past pain that is currently absorbing energy needed to take the next step. Once more, this pattern shows up holographically.

If we assume that people come into their lives to develop certain qualities and learn certain basic lessons,[106] then they will have been drawn to the system they are in as part of that process. In the process running up to the new transformation, then, they will have been moving forward on their path, and are likely to have resolved certain issues as part of that process. When the next change happens, it lays the next challenge before you. The question is whether you recognise that challenge as being part of your path or not. If you don't, you are likely to leave. That may be positive, in that your next challenge lies elsewhere, or you may be avoiding the challenge because it is lighting up something in you that evokes fear. In the latter case, if you leave the system you will simply be confronted with the same challenge in a different context until you engage it and learn what you need to learn.

No wonder, then, that such transitions are so turbulent. Not only are you trying to develop a new organisation, but the individuals involved are going through their own personal transformation at the same time. One way to think about it is that you are being invited to match a higher energetic frequency brought in by the new vision. The beckoning call of this higher frequency reveals, disturbs and dislodges the blockages in your own system that must be transformed, for you to be able to stabilise at the new frequency.

The leader, of course, is the one going through the greatest transformation, being most closely linked to the energy of the system as a whole, as its energetic steward. This can create great confusion in the system, because people's expectations tend to be formed by the perception of leadership most commonly promoted in industrialised society, namely that the leader should always know what to do, be a flawless living example of everything the organisation stands for, and be able to tell everyone else what they should be doing to bring success.

This perception is confusing for the leader themselves: because they can feel the tension and transformation in themselves and they know deep down they do not have all the answers. Nevertheless, they seek to play a role determined by the expectations of the world around them. It is also of course confusing for the community being led: they expect the leader to be stable, well grounded and centred in a time when the leader is going through significant personal transformation parallel to the change in the system, is probably feeling very vulnerable, and is likely to be far from relaxed and in control in the way that their people have grown to expect during the stable phase of the system.

All this is compounded by the uncertainty and fear people are feeling in themselves about the change and their own future, leading them often to project onto the leader their need for stability, inner coherence and relaxed open-heartedness.

An Organisational Case Study

The above thoughts reflect my experience of the actual events unfolding in the development of a real organisation. The organisation in question had been going through the kind of non-linear transformation described above. As part of my vocational training in ECOintention, I had been working energetically with the organisation for a number of months. In the initial scan, the system identified the project as transformation into something new. At that stage, no one was aware of the imminent change that is now underway. The scan also picked up interference from an external entity that could potentially cause division. That interference was likely coming from the exploration of a possible merger with an external party.

The male founding leader of the organisation played a key role in the energetic stewardship of the system as a whole, and his personal transformation is bound to be deeply intertwined with the organisation's development. In the initial scan, the system identified him as one of the stewards, and a woman on the team as the other. Her transformation - and indeed the transformation of the relationship between the two of them - continued to be interwoven with the evolution of the organisation as a whole. If we refer to the pole at the centre of the organisation's torus, one could see the male yang pole and the female yin pole. As developments unfolded, he has been seen as the one reaching for new vision and driving the system towards it, while she has emphasised the grounding of the vision and the connection to what already is. The transformation process of the organisation called both of them into deeper personal exploration of how to hold those yang and yin roles in the healthiest possible ways, and how to hold a creative rather than destructive tension between them. Their individual and collective work influenced the future of the organisation more than most people (would like to) realise. As energetic stewards, it is a parallel journey.

One time when I was with the organisation's team at an event, a number of important things happened. Firstly, there was a moment of surrender by the male leader, when he felt and deeply expressed how he needed to stop fighting against the players in the external party, was ready to forgive them for anything they had done to upset him and to apologise to them for anything he had done to upset them. In this space of vulnerability, a plan was born to approach key players with a gift and try to start afresh. Given the amount of tension there had been between him and the external party, this was quite a step. I could feel the release in my own body as he spoke of his decision. It felt like a strong clearing and relaxation.

However, as is often the case, just when I thought that this meant the merger was now going to work out, the external party started to behave in a way that was totally unacceptable to the organisation's team, and in doing so quite consciously broke a relationship of trust. At that point, it became clear to the male leader and many of us that this was the end of the attempt at merger. A decision was made at that point to end the relationship, but no formal communication was made.

Interestingly, straight after that event, people started to step up from the organisation's community to offer their help and support. It suddenly became clear that the organisation would have to take this next step from its own energy, held in the seed impulse of the organisation itself, and independent of any co-founding partner.

In the twenty-four hours that followed this shift, a plan was born to raise the initial investment from the community itself, ensuring money that was aligned with the values of the system, and at the same time engaging the community in the change process.

Healing started to take place within the organisation's field, in particular between the male and female stewards, as well as with the founder of the original entity which had later morphed into the current organisation. The extent to which past collective and individual traumas are re-integrated determines what energy is available for the system to evolve. It was as if the field of the organisation started to cohere once the flirtation with the other party was clearly at an end. Like the caterpillar in the cocoon, the organisation needed to flex its fragile wings against the other entity to build the strength it needed to fly, gaining greater clarity on its own identity and destiny in the process.

In terms of leadership, the key shift was a release into relationship with all that is. This involved distinguishing healthy yang naming of and striving for a vision from a more destructive energy of battle and struggle. In the healthy dynamic balance, the leader stays in touch with the vision wanting to emerge through them, whilst paying attention to how life is showing it wants to manifest that vision – which is often not how we may have envisaged it. The movement is towards integrating leadership that has traditionally been yang-driven, with the more yin-based community stewardship, as one would expect in the seventh and eighth stages of the octave. Leadership can then emerge through whichever people have the resources and capacities needed at a certain point in time.

Implications

Having explored how volution plays out holographically in the individual and collective dimensions, the next section will explore some examples of specific practices that are in alignment with the volution theory proposed above.

---

1   *Mirabai, in Harvey (1997) p47*

2   *Taegel (2010) p50*

3   *Taegel (2010) p92*

4   *https://catholic.cafe/2020/02/04/what-is-the-tree-of-life-and-why-was-it-guarded-by-the-cherubim/*

5   *Jahn and Dunne (2015) p109*

6   *Jahn and Dunne (2015) p109*

7   *CG Jung (1995) p166*

8   *CG Jung (1995) p263*

9   *Grof, Healing our Deepest Wounds (2011) p187*

10 *Talbot (1991)*

11 *Spangler (2010) p85*

[12] *The Three Initiates, the Kybalion (2006) p60*

[13] *Abram (1996) p217*

[14] *Wilber (1996)*

[15] *Empedocles, in Harvey (1997) p118*

[16] *Stanislav Grof and friends, teleseries (2012)*

[17] *Ray (2001)*

[18] *Abram (1996) p7*

[19] *Merry (2012)*

[20] *Wilber (1996)*

[21] *Graves (2002)*

[22] *Dr Matthijs Schouten and Irene van Lippe, Living in Relationship course (2011), plus co-authored book (2010)*

[23] *Baring (2013)*

[24] *Currivan (personal communication, 2016)*

[25] *Taegel (2010, 2012)*

[26] *From the Isa Upanishad, in Harvey (1997) p39*

[27] *Wilber, Integral Psychology (2000)*

[28] *Currivan (personal communication, 2016)*

[29] *Currivan, The Eighth Chakra (2012)*

[30] *Peter Levine, Waking the Tiger: Healing Trauma (1997)*

[31] *Peter Levine, Waking the Tiger: Healing Trauma (1997)*

[32] *Will Taegel (2010) p29*

[33] *Will Taegel (2010) p80*

[34] *Richard Gardner (1978)*

[35] *Aurobindo, in Harvey (1997) p65*

[36] *David Frawley, in the foreword in Shambhavi Chopra, Kali (2007) xiii*

[37] *Aurobindo, from Savitri, in Harvey (1997) p66*

[38] *Taegel (2010) p79*

[39] *Radin (2013)*

[40] *Roney-Dougal, Where Science and Magic Meet (2010)*

[41] *Currivan (2005, 2017) p140*

[42] *Hans Andeweg (2009, 2011)*

[43] *e.g. Grof (2012), Levine (1997)*

[44] *Currivan (2017)*

[45] *Currivan (2005) p138*

[46] *Currivan (2005) p6-10*

[47] *Laszlo & Currivan (2008) p44*

[48] *Currivan (2017)*

[49] *Currivan (2005) p5*

[50] *Currivan (2017) p114*

[51] *Currivan (personal communication, 2016)*

[52] *Hermes Trismegistus, Copenhaver (1995)*

[53] *Hickman & Taegel (2015)*

[54] *Hawking (2010)*

[55] *e.g. Taylor (2010), Childre & Martin (2000)*

[56] *Grof (2012)*

[57] *see also Kabbal (2006)*

[58] *Dr Taegel, Wild Heart (2010) p10*

[59] *Hans Andeweg (2009, 2011)*

[60] *Machaelle Small Wright (1997)*

[61] *Andeweg (2011) Small Wright (1997)*

[62] *Machaelle Small Wright (1997)*

[63] *Merry (2012)*

[64] *Lao Tzu from the Tao Te Ching, in Harvey (1997) p26*

[65] *CG Jung (1995) p242*

[66] *Journal entry (June 4th 2015)*

[67] *Currivan (2017)*

[68] *Jahn & Dunne (2005)*

[69] *e.g. Currivan (2017)*

[70] *Currivan (2017)*

[71] *Abram (1996) p10*

[72] *CG Jung (1995) p281*

[73] *Talbot (1991) p261*

[74] *Anne Baring (2013)*

[75] *Currivan (2005) p29*

[76] *Schneider (1995)*

[77] *Drunvalo Melchizedek (1990)*

[78] *e.g. Johnson (1997), Pinchbeck (2012)*

[79] *Jahn and Dunne (2015) p92*

[80] *Jahn and Dunne (2015) p94*

[81] *Jahn and Dunne (2015) p96*

[82] *Jahn and Dunne (2015) p110*

[83] *Ruggles (2014), Watson & Keating (1999)*

[84] *Morton & Thomas (1997)*

[85] *Cayce (1968), Cori (2001), Flem-Ath & Wilson (2001), Yoke (1997)*

[86] *Van Daniken (1969)*

[87] *Leviton (2007)*

[88] *https://w.wiki/7wny*

[89] *Bates (2013)*

[90] *Currivan (2017)*

[91] *Calleman (2004, 2009)*

[92] *Currivan (2005) p87*

[93] *Beck & Cowan (1996) p93*

[94] *Laszlo (2001)*

[95] *Andeweg (2009, 2011)*

[96] *Laszlo (2001)*

[97] *Talbot (1991), Rayne (2012)*

[98] *Edmondson (2009)*

[99] *Currivan (2017)*

[100] *Lefferts (2012)*

[101] *Small Wright (1997)*

[102] *Andeweg (2009, 2011)*

[103] *Currivan (2017)*

[104] *Andeweg (2011)*

[105] *see for example the change model in Beck & Cowan (1996)*

[106] *Conrad (2010)*

Chapter Six :
Implications and Practices

The Thesis: *There are practices, both implemented by current communities and documented by the wisdom traditions and today's progressive scientists, that can be used to work with all dimensions of this volution process (beyond merely the part of the spectrum that most of us can analyse).*

"The developing perspective about the cosmic hologram and the fundamental nature of consciousness is finally offering a theoretical context, a 'plausible mechanism' within which to place and perhaps explain supernormal capabilities and occurrences."

Currivan[1]

There is a strong case to be made that humanity and life on Earth are headed towards working more consciously with information* through a volutionary lens. In their book The Sixth Kondratieff, Leo and Simone Nefiodow point to the evidence that the sixth long wave in the global economy (named Kondratieff waves after Nikolai Kondratieff who first published about these cycles) will be primarily driven by *"information flow in and among human beings - physical, psychological, mental,*

---

*   This chapter refers a lot to *"information".* It is important to remember that this term is referring to far more than data. It is referring to the process of things coming into form through intention, literally in-form-ation.

pyscho-mental and social health" as well as *"information flow between human beings, the environment and transcendence - ecological and spiritual health."*[2] They name the reason for this as increasing health problems in individuals and conflict in the social sphere limiting economic potential now and into the future. In order to deal with the challenges ahead, *"psychosocial health"* will be critical: *"the social importance of psychosocial health results from its problem-solving potential."*[3]

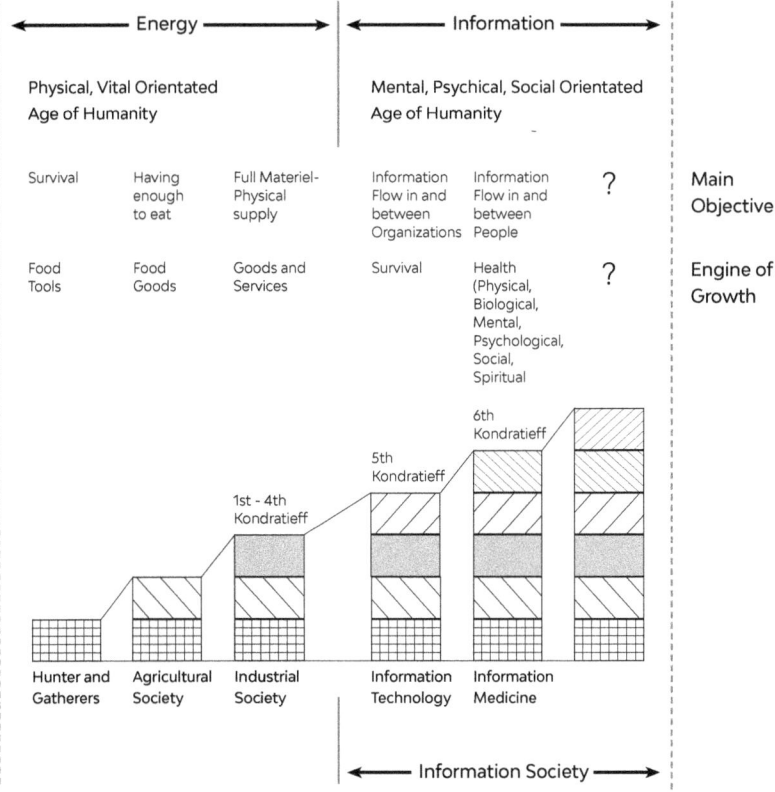

Figure 41 : *Sixth Kondratieff Cycle* (Nefiodow 2014, p108)

This final section focuses on practices, implemented by current communities and documented by the wisdom traditions and today's progressive scientists, that can be used to work with all dimensions of the volution process, using information to increase psychosocial health. In order to engage in the volutionary process beyond the central phases where things manifest in the relative reality we are used to seeing around us, we must develop awareness of and practices for engaging the informational fields and dynamics of energy that make up the other volutionary phases. In this way people become more fully conscious co-creators of life and take into account more of reality when thinking and acting.

Three Perspectives

From a volutionary perspective, between the undifferentiated oneness *"Container"* and the personified I-ness *"Manifest"* - between the wholeness and the *"partness"* of a system - a wide range of dynamics unfold in the relative space. People use many different languages to describe the work they do and the theories that underpin it.

To help clarify the relationships between these different practices and frameworks, I will offer three main perspectives that end up creating different languages and cultures in this area, so we have a code for deciphering the various ways of describing the same context. These perspectives are based on the three personal perspectives: 1st person, 2nd person and 3rd person. The 1st person is the *"I"*: the subjective experience and perspective. The 2nd person I will refer to as *"We"*,[4] because it is really about the interaction between *"I"* and *"You"* in a *"We"* space. The 3rd person is the *"It"* and the apparently objective perspective on something.

Here are some examples of the way these show up in theories and practices around energy and information. In a third person perspective, one would talk about energetic functions, the way information and energy work, similar to the way I have described volution above. All is seen as a system of different interconnecting elements and processes. Richard Leviton[5] describes the various functions he encounters at specific physical sites on the planet - such as connecting different sites and functions to each other, channelling information into matter, protecting certain areas, providing access to certain informational realms.

Hans Andeweg[6] describes specific parameters of a system, such as orgone (life energy), oranur (stressed energy), dor (blocked energy) - these three coming from the work of Wilhelm Reich - grounding, bovis (integration of concept and realisation and POA (Percentage of Organisation and Adaptation). In Andeweg's ECOintention practice, these parameters are measured and used to influence the kind interventions that are made. The third person perspective tends to focus on making pro-active interventions - such as healing a place, in Leviton's work, or balancing an organisation, in Andeweg's work.

In a second person perspective, one would talk not about functions but about other entities or beings that one interacts with - nature spirits, angels and devas, for example. Leviton[7] links the functions he describes to certain entities, such as gnomes, angels and dragons which you engage with when looking to activate certain functions.[8] Small Wright[9] describes ways to work with devas, nature spirits and angels to help co-create a reality that connects your intentions with what is best for life as a whole. She also assigns certain functions to the different entities. The second person perspective tends to focus more on co-creativity with other beings and aspects of life.

In a first person perspective one would talk more about one's inner experience. This is seen more often in receptive practices, where the task is to pick up information intuitively from various channels. In Leviton's workshops, for example, he has people focus on certain locations and report what they feel. Although people may use slightly different language, there is usually a common theme. Gnomes for example create quite a different felt experience than fairies or sylphs. Andeweg also has people feel different energetic qualities and then compare notes inter-subjectively, as part of his four year vocational training in ECOintention.

Person Perspective	1st Person - I	2nd Person - We	3rd Person - It
Quality	Subjective - my inner experience	Inter-subjective - interacting with other beings	Objective - describing and witnessing systems and functions
Examples	Feeling openness, joy, grounded, tension, light-headed, heaviness	Angels, devas, nature spirits, entities	Connecting, Grounding, Protecting, Unlocking, Channeling, Clearing
Focus	Receptive practices	Co-creative practices	Pro-active interventions

Table 7 : *Three Core Perspectives.*

Different people and schools tend to have different preferences for the three perspectives. One will talk in more *"objective"* third person terms about the functions of an energetic system, and may get irritated by *"new-age waffle"* about angels and fairies. Others may feel more comfortable with a second person perspective in the realms of beings and entities, and find the third person too cool, heady and disconnected. Still others may say it's all subjective anyway and you just have to feel it in your own body-mind, a first person perspective.

More often than not, people and schools combine these perspectives to some extent, as we have seen in the examples above. However, it is important to be able to see them as different yet complementary perspectives on the same reality, and it is in that spirit that I will go into more detail on some practices below that explore how to access a fuller spectrum of the volutionary process.

The First Person "I" - Receptivity, Ourselves, Acting on Ourselves

"Can you coax your mind from its wandering/and keep to the original oneness?" the Tao te Ching asks.[10] This points to the place of inner stillness from which we can access field intelligence. The field is a field of information and potential energy, as described in quantum physics. The moment that we observe this *"quantum"* field with our cognitive mind, the potential wave form becomes a coherent wave form, meaning that we can never actually access the quantum potential state with our cognition.[11] This is why we need to still our analytical mind and light

up our more intuitive senses in order to access this field.[12] When our attention is focused on the world of things around us, we pay attention to the disorder and amplify it in our experience. To generate more order in our experience we need to go inside and pay attention to the generative reality. Greater presence creates greater order, allowing life to close the loops of the cycles between order and disorder more quickly, integrating action and awareness, or doing and being, in more rapid feedback loops. The Tao te Ching is essentially a guide to accessing that inner state of being present.

This concept has been popularised in the world of organisational development in recent years by the work of Joseph Jaworski, Peter Senge, Otto Scharmer and Betty Sue Flowers, as what they call *"presencing"*.[13] It is what Scharmer calls the *"blind spot of leadership"*, that ability to find inner stillness and deep knowing that guides us to take wise and better informed decisions.

In Ervin Laszlo's understanding, what he calls the Akashic Field[14] holds all the information that has ever existed and information on the dynamic potentiality of future possibilities. We can access any knowledge we want by attuning ourselves to this field and asking clearly what we want to know. To do this however requires that we activate our intuitive dimension and quiet our rational mind.

The rational mind does have a role in working with information gathered from a field. Such information can come to us in many different forms: sometimes in words, but also in images, feelings or other sensations.

Each individual needs to discover their own intuitive language, and what different sensations actually tell us. This is where the rational mind comes in. Energy has many different qualities and functions, and to be able to interpret, communicate about and work with it, we need to be able to discern those diverse qualities. Working with a shared conceptual framework of energetic terms, such as that developed by Hans Andeweg in his ECOintention practice,[15] enables us to work together in the energetic domain, exchanging our experiences and drawing conclusions.

It is important first to access the sensation through intuition and only thereafter to engage the analytical mind to discern, translate and communicate the experience. This was one of the main lessons learned by Dr Robert Jahn and Brenda Dunne in their 28 years of Princeton Engineering Anomalies Research.[16] They emphasised how important it was to apply their analytical filters only after all the subjective intuitive data had been completely relayed.

Radin[17] refers to the *"inflow of information that we label psi perception, which includes clairvoyance, precognition, and telepathy"*. Serena Roney-Dougal[18] lists out the conditions she discovered in her research that enhanced people's success in accessing this information. They include:

- Relaxation
- Quieting of the analytical mind
- Grounding
- Curiosity
- Openness

These are first-person qualities that create the conditions for receiving information more accurately from the informational fields. There are many practices in the realm of personal development that help develop these qualities, most of which involve some level of directing the attention to inner experience, noticing and accepting the busyness of the mind and the world outside while not getting caught up in it.

One of the most compelling pieces of evidence for the existence of these psi abilities came from a report commissioned by the Congress of the United States in the 1990s from the American Institutes for Research. While producing compelling evidence, the two primary reviewers couldn't agree. Currivan reports:

"The conclusions by the two primary reviewers differed. One, who'd previously been open to the reality of remote viewing, was convinced by the evidence and in favour of then focusing on how such psi phenomena works. The other, previously skeptical, remained unpersuaded. The oversight panel then elaborated a consensus that, while agreeing there was a statistically significant demonstration of the ability to perceive on such a nonlocal basis, there was disagreement as to whether it could be unambiguously attributed to psi or some unconfirmed experimental bias. Without clearly establishing the cause of the proven evidence, the panel also considered that, even if it did exist, the experiments did not identify the origins or nature of the phenomenon."[19]

In other words, while the evidence was there, the members still disputed its validity, regardless of the lack of any proof of error or bias; they couldn't, in any case, understand how it could work.

The Second Person "We" - Co-creativity, en-acting with others

One of the main ways people can co-create with life is by working with attention and intention. The first part of this section explores how that can look when working with other people, and the second explores more examples of co-creating with other entities.

The formative force of life, the force that shapes our material reality, emerges from a process of giving something attention from the heart and bringing in creative intention from the higher mind.[20] If a leader is sensing well from the field, then they have an intuition about which general direction the community is destined to go in order to contribute the piece of the puzzle it holds. With that general direction in mind, it is possible to co-create with life to bring the vision into form, through the conscious use of intention. In this sense, *"leadership"* is grounded in a perspective of co-creation, a continual cycle of sensing and acting.

In his most recent work, The Universe Loves a Happy Ending,[21] Hans Andeweg names ten principles for leading an organisation or stewarding a piece of land in resonance with the energetic architecture of that system:

1. *Check whether your conviction is free and independent - are you really the steward of the entity you lead or are you dependent on others?*

2. *Develop inner tranquillity.*

3. *Become conscious of the whole – hold in your awareness all the different parts of the system you are leading.*

4. *Have a sense of what is happening – a heart-felt connection to the experiences of the people and other life forms in your system.*

5. *Hold your system in the light of love in your heart, including any pain that may be present.*

6. *Affirm and visualise your goals – pay regular attention to your goals, and visualise their realisation.*

7. *Use knowledge and expertise – know about the content of what is being worked on in your system.*

8. *Go with the flow – understand and work with energetic time (such as that described in sacred calendars like that of the Maya, or other fractal systems such as the Elliott timewave).*

9. *Transform your burdened past – be aware of what traumas from the past may be holding the system back from manifesting its purpose and release the energy that is held there.*

10. *Be here now, consciously and with joy – don't take yourself too seriously...*

An important area to explore in the co-creative qualities is working with tensions and seeming polarities. Information fields often show themselves to us through creative tensions. As the intention that we hold as leaders for our system meets the current reality, tensions emerge that invite us towards greater wholeness and coherence. Those tensions can be in the field of relationships between the people in our systems, or around material issues. I like to think of these three architectures in our living systems:

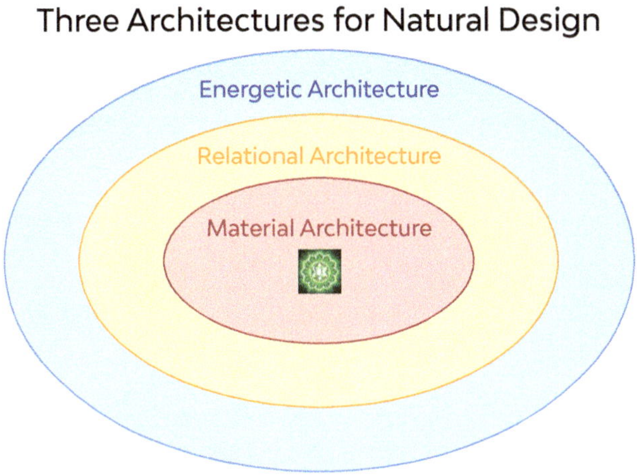

Three Architectures for Natural Design

Figure 42 : *Three Architectures for Natural Design*
(Center for Human Emergence Netherlands 2011)

As we start to align ourselves with the informational and energetic fields, our relational and material architectures are called into resonance with them. That is likely to create tensions in our organisational systems which we need to learn to work creatively with. Practices such as Holacracy's Integrative Decision Making[22] help people in organisations treat tensions as information from the field, and work with that information in such a way that it can be of greatest service to the organisational entity they are leading. The ability for a leader and community to work creatively with tensions is critical, particularly in the increasingly complex and challenging times we live in. Holding a tension open keeps the probability waves open and invites in information and insights from the informational fields to literally in-form how we transcend them.

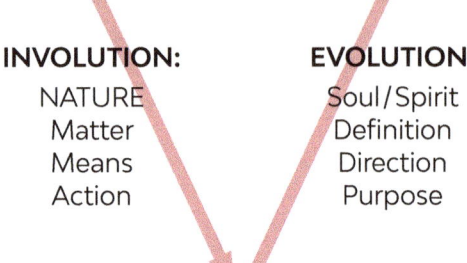

Figure 43 : *The Involution/Evolution Coning Dynamic*
Small Wright (1997, p11)

The remainder of this section about the second person *"We"* perspective looks at co-creation with non-human elements of life. The best example I have encountered of this is Machaelle Small Wright's work on *"Co-creative Science"*.[23] Small Wright has developed a practice that she trialled with a garden, inspired by work at the Findhorn eco-village in Scotland. This practice involves explicit collaboration with entities in the angelic, devic and nature spirit realms.

In the Perelandra process, different players have different co-creative roles. The intention and vision are set by the humans. This is related

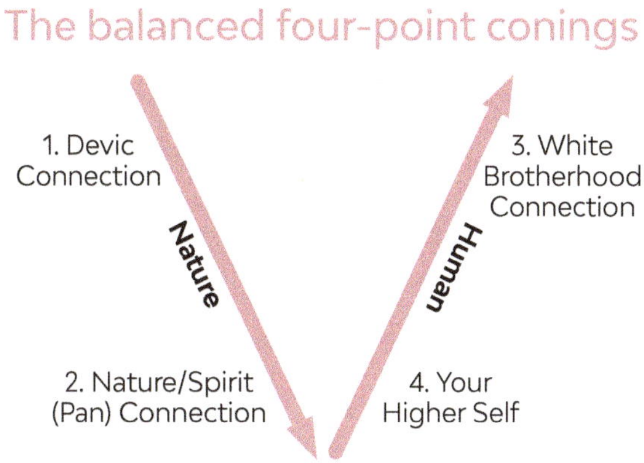

The balanced four-point conings

Figure 44 : *The Balanced Four-Point Conings*
Small Wright (1997, p13)

to the longer-term human transformation process held by an angelic family she calls the White Brotherhood. Together, the humans and the White Brotherhood focus on holding an intention for the future, so that life moves in that general direction: the e-volutionary process.

On the other hand, the blueprint of how to implement such an intention in this reality for the greatest benefit of all life is held by the devas. Pan and the nature spirits are responsible for pulling all the pieces together: the in-volutionary process. Small Wright developed a set of protocols for interacting with these partners to help develop a physical garden or an organisational project (a *"soil-less garden"*), as well as to support healing processes (the Medical Assistance Program).

Roney-Dougal[24] also provides a grounded review of the various elemental nature spirits and the roles they assume. Spangler devotes his book Subtle Worlds to working with the different entities in the subtle realms. He identifies four main ways *"that subtle beings can and do help us"*[25]: firstly, *"by intervening to handle anything we can't handle ourselves yet"*, such as energetic cleansing and transformation; secondly, *"by seeding the realms of thought and feeling with ideas and qualities that human beings can pick up on and be inspired by"*; thirdly, *"by directly offering guidance and instruction to those who can receive it"*; fourthly, *"blending of the presence and energies of the subtle being with those of the incarnate human being in a manner that creates a larger and more potent field than either could manage on his or her own"*.

He also describes how he was given four key practices for working with entities in the subtle realms by his main subtle contact, John: *"attunement to self, attunement to sacredness, attunement to the subtle environment in the physical world around me, and blessing."*[26] An important point he makes from his experience is that communication with the subtle realms works more at a poetic level that needs to be unpacked by the conceptual imagination before the cognitive mind can engage with it.[27]

Spangler describes the subtle realms as *"not so much in the physical sense but conditions and states of consciousness... locations within the vast, universal spectrum of life and sentencing... they are like notes on a guitar string. The plucking of the string creates and sustains the note."*[28]

The Third Person "It" -
Active, Acting on Third Party Systems

"A miracle does not happen in contradiction to nature, but in contradiction to that which is known to us of nature."

Saint Augustine, in Radin[29]

This third-person perspective is maybe the most popularised, due to people's natural tendency in the scientific-rational mindset to orient through the third person. Although the examples of practices below are framed in the third person, they include first- and second-person practices. Radin refers to these practices as the *"outflow of information, which includes psychokinesis and distant healing."*[30]

Abram quotes from anthropological research into the Navajo's view of what we would call *"the future"*. They see it as:

> *"a stock of possibilities, of incompletely realised events and circumstances. They are still most of all 'becoming' (rather than being and involved in the process of 'manifesting' themselves. The human being can, through his thoughts and desire, exert an influence on these 'possibles'."*[31]

Hardy describes how traditional perspectives on quantum physics have polarised into two camps - the indeterministic where it is all random, as postulated by Werner Heisenberg, Niels Bohr and the Copenhagen school, and the deterministic where *"hidden variables"* or an *"implicate order"* determine manifestation on the material or *"explicate"* dimension (postulated by Einstein and David Bohm). She suggests that the underlying reality is closer to the *"synchronistic acausal events"* proposed by Jung and Pauli, where intention and meaning play a role through what she calls *"syg-energy (semantic energy)"*[32]

The practice I am most familiar with which reflects this perspective is that of ECOintention, developed by Hans Andeweg and Rijk Bols.[33] This practice was originally known as ECOtherapy and grew out of resonance therapy, which itself emerged from radionics, as developed in the 1920s at Stanford University in California. All three methods use treatments (or *"balancing"*) at a distance through a map or photograph. I focus on ECOintention not only because of my experience of it, but also because of the 20 years of application and related research conducted around it. From the various practices I am aware of, this is one of the most developed and researched in terms of impact on larger scale systems such as natural parks and organisations. Towards the end of the section I will mention some other practices in this area.

ECOintention

The different methods that developed into ECOintention have become less technical with each step. In radionics, only radionic equipment was used. In resonance therapy symbols and fractals (mathematical images and formulae) were added. An ECOintention Practitioner uses no radionic equipment at all, but has a self-assembled energetic toolkit including colours, crystals, homeopathic treatments, Bach flower remedies, symbols and an orgone beamer. It is important that the owner, manager or guardian of the project be intensely involved in the ECOintention balancing process. That is not the case in radionics or resonance therapy.

Before proceeding it is important to define certain terms used here. In ECOintention, the *"Guardian"* is the person who is ultimately responsible for a certain entity. That could be the warden of a piece of land or the head of a business unit or organisation. It could also be more than one person if a group is collectively accountable.

The Guardian(s) may not always be the people one would expect and are checked in the initial informational scan by the ECOintention Practitioner. The *"Practitioner"* is the ECOintention-trained person working at a distance on the project. The *"Coach"* works directly with the *"Guardian"*, helping them to steward their project in the context of the informational data they are receiving. The Coach role could also be played by the person performing the Practitioner role. The *"Client"* is often the Guardian, the person who contracts the ECOintention Practitioner and Coach to carry out the work.

Below is a short description of the different steps of an ECOintention project, taken from an adapted translation of material from the Dutch ECOintention website. The ECOintention process essentially creates a non-physical attractor that increases the probability of a project achieving its goals and fulfilling its purpose.

An ECOintention project varies from 7 to 12 months, depending on the size and complexity of the project. How long the energy stays at its target levels, as defined by the ECOintention practice, depends on the attention and intention of the Guardian.

ECOintention uses a set of parameters to measure the information and energetic data of a system. The vitality of a living system is measured by:

- how grounded it is (% grounding).

- how adequately its own information field is integrated (Bovis scale).

- how fit it is with its context (% organisation and adaptation - POA).

- how much life energy is present (% orgone).

- how much blocked and stressed energy is present (% dor & oranur).

These parameters are measured by the Practitioner dowsing (more below). Over the years, specific target values for each of these parameters have emerged as being key for a well-balanced informational energetic architecture.

Before the Practitioner intervenes in any way, the Guardian needs to have clearly identified the scope of the project: what are the goals, exactly which entity, within what timeframe? There needs to be a time-space container in which the information and energy can land. The clearer and more focused the scope, the greater the chance of success. Like drawing back the string on the bow: the tighter and steadier it is, the surer the arrow will fly. From the scientific perspective of Laszlo and Currivan,[34] the greater the initial degree of order in a system (and therefore the lower its initial informational entropy), the greater the system's propulsion and the greater the opportunity for additional informational entropy (differentiation and interconnection) and manifestation.

Therefore, the clearer the identity and boundaries of the project at the outset, the more effective an ECOintention intervention is likely to be and the greater the possibilities of success for the project itself.

1 : Energetic Scan

After the first meeting between the ECOintention Practitioner and the Client, the Practitioner completes an energetic scan of the organisation or ecosystem. This will reveal the vitality of the project, whether the Guardian's goals are achievable and how long it will take to get the project aligned energetically.

For this scan (and the subsequent balancing interventions) the ECOintention Practitioner uses a *"resonator"* - a map, floor plan or the name of the project - through which to establish an intuitive connection with the morphic field containing the blueprint of the project. At this stage, the Practitioner is using receptive competencies to read the information in the membrane (informational field) of the organism.

The initial scan takes place at three levels:

i. **Concept Level** : where the vision, mission, resulting goals and strategy of the organisation are determined. The organisation is lead from this level, which can be seen as the organisation's head, where the thinking is based. From a volutionary perspective, this relates to the seed and potential.

ii. **Realisation Level** : the workplace or operational level. This is the place of action and turnover, where words are turned into deeds, where ideas are implemented and transformed into products and services. It is similar to the stomach.

In an ecosystem this is where the life processes take place. This is the central part of the volutionary process where the information is most fully expressed as energy and matter.

iii. **Middle Level** : where internal and external communication happens, the interaction within the organisation and with other organisations and its operating environment. It can be compared to the heart, to feeling.

It is also the domain of branding and public relations. Blockages or low-energy at this level can often lead to miscommunication and misunderstanding. This field is located just outside the central systems of the volutionary process, where the system is resonating both inside and outside.

2 : Conversations between the Client and the Practitioner

Graphics with the energetic data from the scan provide information about blockages, stress, healthy life energy and the degree of self-organisation of the project. The data is compared to the target values of a healthy, self-organising organisation or ecosystem.

This visual presentation gives the Client an immediate insight into the state of the whole system. The scan also shows to what extent their goals can be achieved using ECOintention. The next step is a proposal and an outline of the costs. Once agreement is reached with the Client, the balancing project can start.

3 : Making a Holon

Before the ECOintention Practitioner tests for a balancing, they shrink the project map to a couple of centimetres in diameter and create a holon - an energetic resonance box - around it, represented by an unbroken circular line. This optimises the project's healthy vibration, connecting the volutionary seed to the potential so that all the information related to the system is available.

4 : Testing for a Balancing

Using the holon and intuition, the ECOintention Practitioner establishes contact with the project, *"asking"* it what it needs to strengthen its own healthy vibration. Everything is energy and everything has its own unique vibration. The ECOintention Practitioner strengthens the unique vibration of the project using things with a similar vibration, offered from the Practitioner's energetic toolkit, such as colours, crystals, music, mandalas, symbols, Bach flower remedies, homeopathy. The balancing of vibrations in this way removes blockages, harmonises stress, adds healthy life energy and increases the project's self-organising capacity. Here, the Practitioner is using receptive skills to pick up information from the organism's membrane.

5 : Balancing

A balancing consists of a number of steps carried out several times per week. Depending on the results of the latest scan, colours, mandalas, music, symbols, Bach flower remedies or other informational energetic interventions are used. The ECOintention Practitioner places each item in a specific position on the holon. This placing connects the project's information fields and the specific informational intervention with each other.

It is an art that takes practice and experience. This is the moment the transfer of energy and information takes place. During the balancing the Guardian concentrates on their affirmations, thereby giving the energy direction. This unique collaboration improves the speed and quality of the developments. Here, the Practitioner is using active skills to interact with the organism. See below for a list of conditions for successful active practice.

6 : Project Support

Every 9 to 14 days the project is tested for new balancing with an energetic scan. The scan shows whether the energetic values are increasing and the project improving. The results of the new scan are presented in a chart and sent with a report to the Guardian.

The ECOintention Coach visits the project every 4 to 6 weeks, meeting with the Guardian to assess progress and conduct energetic check-ups. Where necessary, the affirmations are amended and heavily-stressed areas can receive healing on location. The Guardian is coached in the principles of resonant leadership, so that once the process is completed they can manage the energy themselves. This brings the Guardian's energy more into resonance with a volutionary perspective, so they can lead the system from a more informed place.

7 : ECOintention in 3 Phases

i. Balancing

After 4 to 8 months the energetic target values of a healthy organisation are reached. The time needed is dependent on the size and complexity of the project. The reason it takes this long is not due to the time required to change the energetic values - that can happen instantly. It is due to the amount of time it takes for human and other organic life forms to integrate the new information. This phase essentially involves working in the information fields outside the central manifest volutionary system.

ii. Stabilising

In the stabilising phase, the energy of the project is maintained at the target levels. This allows all parts of the project the time they need to absorb and integrate the energy. A lot of changes can happen in the project during this phase. The ECOintention Practitioner must stay in touch with the project and the Guardian during this phase, when the new information is finding ways to express itself concretely, in energy and matter, in the project.

iii. Continuation

After 3 to 6 months the stabilisation phase moves into the continuation phase. The energy is now well anchored throughout the project. All elements are well aligned. The ECOintention Practitioner steps back and the Guardian takes over full stewardship of the project. After a while, they can request an energetic check-up scan, and some short balancing interventions can be carried out where necessary.

8 : ECOintention Results

The Client's goals determine the results of the ECOintention practice. In most of the projects the goals are realised. Given the broad diversity of goals, many different results have been achieved, including:

- Increasing assignments and revenue.

- Improved organisation and collaboration.

- Higher profit and better financial results.

- More free time and inner relaxation for the Guardian.

- Healthier staff, animals, trees and plants.

- Better harvest and quality of product.

- Increased biodiversity.

Research Findings after 4 Years of Research

A four-year research project into the effects of ECOintention showed that managers and Guardians have more time to themselves, are more relaxed and more effective at realising their goals. Organisations enjoy better organisation, communication, productivity and finances. The research was carried out in 2014, 2008, 2007 and 2005 in projects run by the third and fourth year trainees in the vocational program to become an ECOintention Practitioner.

Research Methodology

To research the impact of ECOintention, the Guardians were given a questionnaire with 11 statements about their wellbeing and the condition of their organisation or project, at the start of the project and after 4, 8 and 12 months. For example: *"I have time for myself", "I achieve my goals", "My organisation's finances are healthy".*

The Guardians assigned each statement a score of 1 to 7, depending on to what extent they agreed with the statement. In this way their opinions at the start and at the end of the project could be compared.

Significant Results

The 2014 research showed that for all statements the score increased compared to the beginning of the ECOintention project.

For 67% of the statements the increase was statistically significant. The results were similar in 2005, 2007 and 2008. The 4-year research shows that managers and Guardians experience improvements in many areas for themselves and their organisations/ecosystems at the end of an ECOintention process. They have more time to themselves, are more relaxed, have greater self-confidence, feel healthier and are better at achieving their goals. In their organisation or project, they experience greater organisational coherence and better communication. Productivity increases and finances improve.

Question	T1 (n=31)	T2 (n=31)	T3 (n=31)	T4 (n=31)
I have time for myself.	3,5	3,9	**4,5**	**4,7**
I am relaxed.	3,9	4,6	**4,9**	**5,1**
The organization is acheiving its goals.	3,5	**4,1**	**5,0**	**4,6**
Communication with the outside world.	4,1	4,4	**4,8**	**5,1**
Financial health of the organization.	3,3	3,5	**4,2**	**4,2**
I feel self-confident.	5,0	5,3	**5,7**	**5,7**
Communication in the organization.	4,4	4,5	5,0	**5,1**
Luck is on my side.	4,5	4,4	**5,4**	4,9
The organization of the enterprize.	4,4	4,2	**5,1**	4,8
I'm at the hub of my organization.	5,3	5,2	5,7	5,4
I'm healthy.	5,3	5,3	5,7	5,4

Table 8 : *ECOintention results in 2014: the questionnaire was completed by 31 Guardians at four moments in the process. Green means a higher and red means a lower score than the initial measurement. Figures in bold represent a statistically significant change. The scale was 1 (poor) to 7 (very good).*
Source: Center for ECOintention (2014)

From a volutionary perspective, we can conclude that the ECOintention process is informationally entropic for the system it works with: creating greater differentiation and interconnectedness at the same time, increasing its fit with its context and purpose.

While Andeweg and colleagues talk about the ECOintention practice in terms of energy, from a volutionary perspective it is more accurate to think of it as information expressed as energy. Energy is dynamic, moving information, whereas manifest matter is information fixed in standing waves.

Further Examples of the Third-Person Perspective in Action

The third-person perspective is important in that it identifies and clarifies the boundaries of the entity being worked with. Being clear on the boundaries of what we are working with is essential, because information is stored in the membrane of the entity. Energy needs a defined boundary to be able to work. As Currivan says:

> *"Where waves are free to move, they will do so until their energy eventually dissipates. But where waves are generated, for example, in a closed space or by stroking the strings of a musical instrument whose ends are fixed, the waves are not free to travel and instead set up standing patterns of vibration."* [35]

Being clear on which *"closed space"* or identity we are engaging with, and seeing it as existing outside ourselves, is an important aspect of setting up the We relationship. There needs to be clarity of both the I and the It to establish the most free and effective interaction.

Given that many entities contain stressed or blocked energy, it is important for the energetic Practitioner to create clear boundaries between self and the entity, to prevent the energy from jumping over into one's system.

As we shall see, this means not that there is no first- or second-person resonance, but that there is clarity about what energy belongs to which entity, and its particular journey.

In CosMos, Laszlo and Currivan describe a number of experiments that seemed to demonstrate the power of intention. For example, the work of William Turner and a group of experienced meditators:

> *"Over a number of years, they have successfully imprinted intentions to either increase or decrease the acidity of purified water above or below its previous predicted level. In other tests, they printed the intention to alter the speed of development of fruit-fly larvae. In every case and over many different experiments, the results have been replicated and have shown significant variations from the norm – always in the direction of the given intention."* [36]

In The Wave, [37] Currivan documents the research into the effectiveness of energetic and PSI interventions, as does Dean Radin in Supernormal. [38] The impact of transcendental meditation on violent crime rates is one of the most well known - with a maximum of 23.3% decrease as compared to the same period in previous years, with 500 million to 1 odds against this being chance. [39]

Both Currivan and Radin link the external impact to internal states of the practitioners. Roney-Dougal[40] summarises the qualities required for effective active energetic interventions that her research turned up:

- Focus on the end-result, not on the process of how it is achieved.

- Don't be too serious; light-heartedness and fun work best.

- Impact seems to happen after one has finished trying, the release-of-effort effect.

- Group work can help get round any disbelief that you are making it happen.

After documenting much of the research, Laszlo and Currivan conclude that *"all these results support the view that the effects of nonlocal influence relate to the intensity of the intention, the level of mental and emotional coherence of group, and its size."*[41]

Radin and Dunne note that *"reports from our operators suggested that successful results also required that they establish an emotional connection with the tasks at hand, a relationship we have come to refer to as 'resonance'."*[42]

"And we often noted that when the dynamic interaction among the PEAR staff members was at its warmest and most collaborative, experimental results appear to reflect this residence with stronger and more consistent results."[43]

There is one final important point to make about our ability to (co-creatively) impact reality through our work with the informational and energetic dimensions. Ken Wilber[44] describes twenty tenets of holons (the parts and wholes of all life). Tenet number six is *"The lower sets the possibilities of the higher; the higher sets the probabilities of the lower"*. The lower levels of a holon are closer to matter, and the higher levels get increasingly subtle. This implies that the more physical reality will ultimately determine the parallel possibilities in the more subtle dimensions, whereas the subtle dimensions can only increase probabilities in the material world.

While the kind of work described above can therefore never guarantee impact in the physical world, it can nevertheless increase the probability of a certain outcome manifesting. As Jahn and Dunne conclude after their 28 years of research at Princeton University, *"the accumulation of small effects can compound to significant shift in the mean of the statistical distribution of random events."*[45]

Nassim Haramein's work in the world of physics reinforces how this might work from that perspective. He states that spacetime isn't just a gravitational dent or a gravity well in the universe but that there is a *"torque"* in the well that makes it curl and spin. It what he calls *"Einstein with a twist"*. He states that the torque that causes spin comes from changes in density. A tension between current (gross) and desired (subtle) reality would be equivalent to a change in density. That would trigger the voluntary manifestation process.

"Torque is a force that tends to rotate or turn things. You generate

a torque any time you apply a force using a wrench. Tightening the lug nuts on your wheels is a good example. When you use a wrench, you apply a force to the handle. ... To calculate the torque, you just multiply the force by the distance from the centre."

In physics, the greater the distance, the greater the torque. In consciousness, the more clearly felt the volutionary tension, in other words the greater the felt psychological distance between current and desired reality, the greater the *"torque"* which leads to a stronger spin and intenser manifestation process with a higher probability of success. In organisational decision-making, for example, it is good practice to really deepen the collective understanding and feeling of an existing tension as that increases the likelihood of an adequate solution emerging.[46]

Laszlo & Currivan[47] describe how different types of entities have a *"biofield"* that determines the range of possibilities it can draw from (e.g. the heights of people). Within that field of possibilities, working in information and energy fields can increase the probabilities of a certain possibility manifesting. This perspective enables us to connect the concepts of predestination and free will.

Spangler describes this relationship from his more second person perspective:

"All things being equal, if a physical person has a strong intention to do something and is using his or her will to see that it's done, he or

she will exert a much more powerful influence within the physical world than a comparable nonphysical being trying to will this person to stop and not do that thing.

"The physical person is in resonance with physical activity and energy, whereas the subtle being is not... It can (only) attempt to influence the fields of subtle energy within a particular physical environment to influence probabilities."[48]

Integrating the Three Perspectives

The very idea of matter as an expression of consciousness, which these kind of approaches reflect, has been embraced by top physicists. Max Planck was clear: *"I regard consciousness as fundamental. I regard matter as derivative from consciousness."[49]* Currivan herself emphasises the need for *"coherent intensity"* to increase influence,[50] linking the impact of any intervention we make to our interior states. She goes on to describe it in this way:

"In scientific terms, the resonance of our attention and intention causes the quantum field of free-wave possibilities to harmonise into the coherent standing waves of realised materiality.

"The higher our vibrational awareness, the more focused our attention and the more coherent our intention, the greater our empowerment to consciously co-create sustained health and well-being."[51]

Linking a third-person perspective to a first- and second-person perspective, she notes:

"For a holographic projection to create a three-dimensional hologram, the light source needs to be coherent. And for the holographic principle to create the physical world, the coherent intention of higher consciousness is required."[52]

From a holographic perspective, this implies that changing something in one place impacts everything. In the words of Braden:

"Just as a hologram contains the original image in all of its many parts, any change made to just one of those segments becomes reflected everywhere throughout the pattern."[53]

Other practices with similar intentions are well documented by Currivan, Currivan & Laszlo, Hardy, Radin, Roney-Dougal and Talbot.[54] Radin,[55] for example, documents research showing how people who believe in their ability to do something perform better than those who don't - the first-person beliefs influencing the third-person behaviour. As Wolfgang Pauli noted, *"It is my personal opinion that in the science of the future, reality will neither be 'psychic' nor 'physical' but somehow both and somehow neither."*[56]

The entanglement of the observer and observed has been the domain not only of quantum physics, but also of philosophy, with Merleau-Ponty's work suggesting that *"participation is a defining attribute of perception itself"*:

"By asserting that perception, phenomenologically considered, is inherently participatory, we mean that perception always involves,

at its most intimate level, the experience of the active interplay, or coupling, between the perceiving body and that which it perceives."[57]

This leads Abram to state: *"we are all animists"*. He goes on to describe how the Uto-Aztecan and Athapaskan language groups make no clear distinction between space and time but rather *"a subtle differentiation between manifest and unmanifest spatiality – that is, a sense of space as a continual emergence from implicit to explicit existence, and human intention as participant with this encompassing emergence."*[58] It is indeed in the present moment that all the perspectives are united:

"That which has been and that which is to come are not elsewhere – they are not autonomous dimensions independent of the encompassing present in which we dwell. They are, rather, the very depths of this living place–hidden depths of its distances and a concealed depth on which we stand."[59]

Invitation

At the very end of the DVD reporting on their 28 years of inquiry into these matters at the Princeton Engineering Anomalies Research project, Bob Jahn[60] concluded that they had proven beyond statistical doubt that human intention impacts the world around us, and that it was now up to us to work out the implications.

In the context of seeing life through the lens of volution, we see the importance of this ability in influencing formative phases of the life process that have until now generally remained outside our awareness. The pioneers in this area, only a handful of whom I have been able to describe in this section, have given us much to work with. The opportunity now exists to build on their experience, work more consciously with the whole volutionary process and bring this awareness and practice into the mainstream. As Talbot put it:

"As we become more adept at tinkering with what Jahn and Dunne call the interface between consciousness and its environment, is it possible for us to experience reality that is once again malleable?

"If this is true, we will need to learn much more than we presently know to manipulate such a plastic environment safely, and perhaps that is one purpose of the evolutionary processes that seem to be unfolding in our midst." [61]

---

[1] *Currivan (2017) p200*

[2] *Leo and Simone Nefiodow, The Sixth Kondratieff (2014) p31*

[3] *Leo and Simone Nefiodow, The Sixth Kondratieff (2014) p61*

[4] *in the tradition of Ken Wilber (1995)*

[5] *Richard Leviton (2005, 2007)*

[6] *Hans Andeweg (2009, 2011)*

[7] *Leviton (2005, 2007)*

[8] *Merry (2011b)*

[9] *Small Wright (1997)*

[10] *Lao Tzu (1999)*

[11] *Talbot (1991)*

[12] *Andeweg (2009)*

[13] *Senge et al (2004)*

[14] *Laszlo (2004)*

[15] *Andeweg (2009)*

[16] *Jahn & Dunne (2005)*

[17] *Radin (2013) p271*

[18] *Serena Roney-Dougal (2010)*

[19] *Currivan (2017) p198*

[20] *Andeweg (2009)*

[21] *Andeweg (2016) p207-215*

[22] *Robertson (2015)*

[23] *Small Wright (1997)*

[24] *Roney-Dougal (2010) p170-199*

[25] *Spangler, Subtle Worlds (2010) p26-28*

[26] *Spangler, Subtle Worlds (2010) p37*

[27] *Spangler, Subtle Worlds (2010) p43*

[28] *Spangler, Subtle Worlds (2010) p61*

[29] *Saint Augustine, in Radin (2013) p46*

[30] *Radin (2013) p271*

[31] *Abram (1996) p192-193*

[32] *Hardy (2008) p322-323*

[33] *Andeweg (2009, 2016)*

[34] *Laszlo and Currivan (2008) p61*

[35] *Currivan (2005) p90*

[36] *Laszlo and Currivan (2008) p196*

[37] *Currivan, The Wave (2005) p123-157*

[38] *Dean Radin, Supernormal (2013) p130-275*

[39] *Dean Radin, Supernormal (2013) p204*

[40] *Roney-Dougal (2010)*

[41] *Laszlo and Currivan (2008) p92*

[42] *Radin and Dunne (2015) p106*

[43] *Radin and Dunne (2015) p107*

[44] *Ken Wilber (1995)*

[45] *Jahn and Dunne (2015) p119*

[46] *https://resonancescience.org*

[47] *Laszlo & Currivan (2008) p65*

[48] *Spangler (2010) p25*

[49] *quoted in Currivan (2017)*

[50] *Currivan (2005) p132*

[51] *Currivan (2005) p133*

[52] *Currivan (2005) p287*

[53] *Braden (2007) p109*

[54] *Currivan (2005, 2017), Currivan & Laszlo (2008), Hardy (2008), Radin (2013), Roney-Dougal (2010), Talbot (1991)*

[55] *Radin (2013) p89*

[56] *Radin (2013) p311*

[57] *Abram (1996) p57*

[58] *Abram (1996) p193*

[59] *Abram (1996) p216*

[60] *Bob Jahn (2005)*

[61] *Talbot (1991) p300*

Conclusion

The process of working on this book has taken me into the depths of both my mind and my being. The act of researching material that points so clearly towards a dynamically interconnected Universe, where the boundaries of our inner and outer worlds are so subtle, is bound to be psycho-active.

The process of reading, reflecting and writing has impacted profoundly my sense of who I am and my experience of my relationship to the world around me. The bigger and more beautiful the picture that emerges from my mind, the more crystalline and grounded is my experience of life.

Each new discovery of course opens new doors, as explored in the Further Research section below. At the same time, I do feel a wholeness and completion around this volution thesis. This new philosophical argument about the holographic and trans-linear dynamics of life feels right, as well as adding up rationally.

As ever, this step will be a foundation for the next steps.

Further Research

There are two main questions that still play around in my mind related to this thesis. They are connected through the idea of perspective. The first is about our place in the volution of our Universe, and the second relates to our perspective of our Universe itself.

One of the questions I came across regularly in my literature review and general material in this domain is how it is that the Universe has actually unfolded with just the right conditions to create life as we experience it, and that we seem to be right in the middle of the scale.

Here are some quotes to illustrate this:

"We human beings literally stand midway on the scale between the nuclear and Galactic realms."

Laszlo & Currivan[1]

"The measures of physical constants or relationships between forces need to be exactly what they are otherwise our Universe would have been snuffed out before it even got going; dying at its first challenge of creating balances between energy and matter or perishing before the first stars were formed."

Currivan[2]

"As we continue our journey of exploration of our perfect Universe and ultimately what it means to be human, the number N also ensures that we are poised midway in size between a molecule and a star; held in the benevolent balance of these cosmic forces which have shaped us."

Currivan[3]

"Mankind is poised midway between the gods and beasts."

Plotinus in Wilber[4]

Figure 45 illustrates the point.:

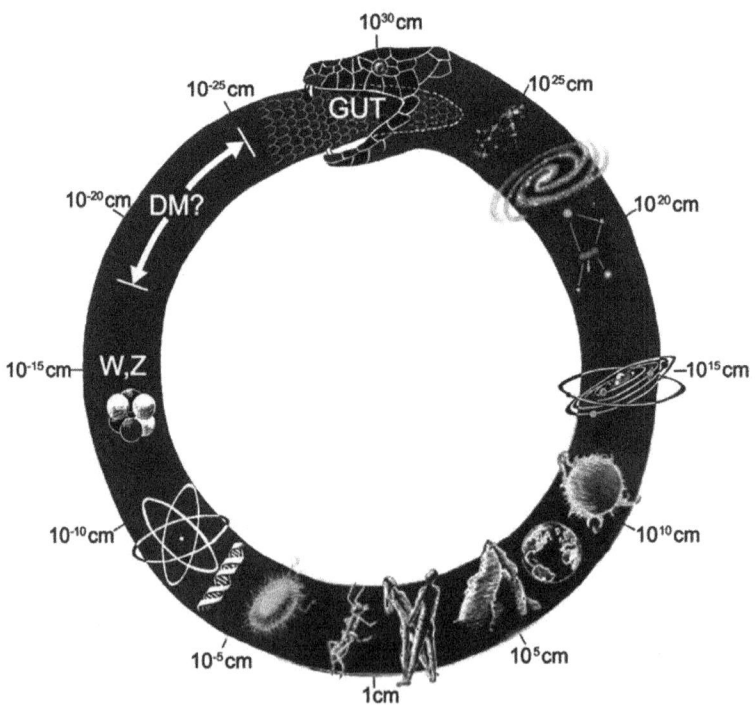

Figure 45 : *The Cosmic Uroboros*   (Source : Discover Magazine)

The perspective that holds that this is such a miracle has never sat comfortably with me, not because it is not true that the parameters that need to be in place for life to have evolved this way are very specific, but more because it seems obvious if one looks at it from a consciousness perspective.

Given all the evidence quoted above that our inner and outer worlds co-arise, surely at any moment we are at the very centre of our own volutionary process, held in the creative tension field of our own seed-potential envelop. Our apparent past and future will be equally balanced as they are the equivalent of the branches and roots of a tree that grow out simultaneously to ensure the tree is balanced.

The further we look into space the deeper we will be able to look into matter and vice-versa. It is as if our awareness expands in all directions of time and space from our own centre. As individuals, we are a holographic aspect, microcosmic co-creators, me and we reflected as one. Therefore the idea that it is a miracle that we are who and what we are now, seems to me to be an inadequate way of thinking about it. It seems obvious that everything has come together in a perfect relationship for us to be who and where we are now - or else we wouldn't be here... That notion is calling me to further contemplation.

Another question that has arisen for me concerns the relative perspective of what a closed and open system is. In our current perspective, as described above in the volution thesis, all systems are open up to the level of our Universe, which is a closed system so all energy-matter is conserved on a physicalised level. It seemed strange to me that this wasn't a fractal and, reflecting on it, I concluded that this might have to with our relative perspective.

Currently, the boundary within which we can make sense of our reality is our own Universe. We have not yet developed a perspective capable of sitting outside our Universe and looking at it in relationship to other Universes, for example.

I still wonder whether our understanding of our Universe as a closed system is related to our perspective of having chosen our Universe as our macro-boundary for now, and whether, if we were able to conceive if it as part of a bigger whole, our understanding would change to it being an open system, with our closed system criteria shifting to the next greatest whole that we could conceive of (a multi-verse, for example).

---

[1] *Laszlo & Currivan (2008) p111*

[2] *Currivan (2017) p85*

[3] *Currivan (2017) p87*

[4] *Plotinus in Wilber (1982) p162*

Purpose

Since I wrote the original manuscript I have started trying to explain pieces of volution to people and it has actually been resonating very well. It is making me realise that the time is indeed right for a more holistic understanding of life that goes beyond the linearity of our evolutionary perspective and makes space for the subtle information and energy dimensions that the latest science is pointing to.

It is more whole, shows why the challenge of reconnecting to ourselves as the Earth is so critical and opens up a common language for exploring new ways of healing our relationship to ourselves, each other and the rest of the planet.

It's time.

Next Steps

The next steps I see myself taking in relationship to this thesis involve both the inner and outer journey.

My experience of writing this has been like an inquiry, an opening through which insights have poured. It feels almost like a channelling process. I know that if someone asked me to sit down and explain the volution theory to them in detail, it wouldn't come across as very coherent. I need to go back and carefully read what "I" have written until it really resonates with my system as a whole and enters my full being. I know it holds significant implications for my work in the world and these will start to manifest themselves as this concept drops deeper into my awareness.

Part of that process is also putting it out there in the world for people to engage with, question, deepen and further explore - which is the impulse behind this book. The original dissertation is on **volutiontheory.net** with a blog of latest insights and connections.

Ultimately I trust that this process I went through, and continue to go through, is of service to life as a whole, as we become more conscious of our wholeness, uniqueness and interconnectedness all at the same time.

So be it.

@peterdacremerry

peter merry

peter merry

@PeterDMerry

peterdmerry

petermerry@ubiquityuniversity.org

petermerry.org

volutiontheory.net

ubiquityuniversity.org

References

Abram, D. (1996). *The Spell of the Sensuous.* New York, Random House.

Anasazi (2012). *Magnetism.* Retrieved from cropcircleconnector.com/anasazi/fringe2012g.html

Andeweg, H. (2009). *In Resonance with Nature.* Edinburgh, Floris Books.

Andeweg, H. (2011). *Scheppend Leven.* Cothen, Juwelenschip.

Andeweg, H. (2016). *The Universe Loves a Happy Ending.* New York, Hunter House.

Artress, L. (2006). *Walking a Sacred Path.* New York, Riverhead Trade.

Baring, A. (2013). *The Dream of the Cosmos.* Dorset, Archive Publishing.

Barr, F. (2006). *The Theory of Evolutionary Process as a Unifying Paradigm.* Retrieved from arthuryoung.com/barr.html.

Bates, B (2013). *The Way of Wyrd.* London, Hay House.

Bateson, G. (1979). *Mind and Nature.* New York, Bantam.

Bearden, T. (2003). *The Importance of Leyton's Hierarchies of Symmetry.* Retrieved from cheniere.org/techpapers/leyton.htm.

Beck & Cowan (1996). *Spiral Dynamics.* Oxford, Blackwell.

Bekenstein, J. D. (August 2003). *Information in the Holographic Universe.* Scientific American, 289 (2), p58-65.

Binder, T. (1995). *In the Wave Lies the Secret of Creation.* Waynesboro, the University of Science and Philosophy.

Bloom, H. (2000). *Global Brain.* Toronto, John Wiley & Sons.

Bohm, D. (1980). *Wholeness and the Implicate Order.* London, Routledge and Kegan Paul.

Boltzmann, L. (1866). *"Über die Mechanische Bedeutung des Zweiten Hauptsatzes der Wärmetheorie".* Wiener Berichte. 53: p195–220.

Braden, G. (2007). *The Divine Matrix.* London, Hay House.

Calleman, C.J. (2004). *The Mayan Calendar and the Transformation of Consciousness.* Rochester, Vermont, Bear & Company.

Calleman, C.J. (2009). *The Purposeful Universe.* Rochester, Vermont, Bear & Company.

Carpenter D. & Sarelas M. (2010). *The Torus, the Vortex and the Vacuum.* Retrieved from light-weaver.com/vortex/1vortex.html

Castillo, M. (March 2012). *"The Omega Point and Beyond: The Singularity Event".* American Journal of Neuroradiology. 33 (3): 3935.

Cayce, E. (1968). *Edgar Cayce on Atlantis.* New York, Warner.

Center for ECOintention (2004). ECOintention Research 2014.
Marl, Center for ECOintention.

Childre D. & Martin H. (2000). *The Heartmath Solution.*
New York City, HarperOne.

Chopra, S.L. (2007). *Yogic Secrets of the Dark Goddess.*
New Delhi, Wisdom Tree.

Chown, M. (15 January 2009). *Our world may be a giant hologram.*
NewScientist, 2691, p24-27.

Clements, J., Ettling, D., Jenett, D., & Shields, L. (1998).
Organic research: *Feminine spirituality meets transpersonal research.*
In W. Braud & R. Anderson, *Transpersonal research methods for
the social sciences: Honoring human experience* (p114-127).
Thousand Oaks, CA, Sage.

Cohen, A. (2011). *Evolutionary Enlightenment.* New York, Select Books.

Conrad, E.D. (2010). *A New Dawn Awaits.* Sandy UK, Bright Pen.

Copenhaver, B. (ed.), Trismegistus, H, Asclepius, (1995).
Hermetica: The Greek Corpus Hermeticum and the Latin Asclepius.
Cambridge, Cambridge University Press.

Cori, P. (2001). *Atlantis Rising.* Lincoln, Authors Choice Press.

Currivan, J. (2005). *The Wave.* Ropley, O Books.

Currivan, J. (2011). *Hope: Healing Our People and Earth.* London, Hay House.

Currivan, J. (2012). *The 8th Chakra.* London, Hay House.

Currivan, J. (2016). *Our in-formed and holographic Universe.* Powerpoint Presentation.

Currivan, J. (2017). *The Cosmic Hologram.* Rochester, Inner Traditions.

Doczi, G. (2005). *The Power of Limits – Proportional Harmonies in Nature, Art and Architecture.* London, Shambhala.

Edmondson, A. (2009). *A Fuller Explanation.* Colorado, EmergentWorld LLC Productions.

Elgin, D. (1993). *Awakening Earth.* New York, William Morrow and Company Inc.

Flem-Ath R. & Wilson C. (2001). *The Atlantis Blueprint.* London, Sphere.

Fuller, R. (1975). Synergetics: *The Geometry of Thinking.* New York, Macmillan.

Gardner, R. (1978). *Evolution Through the Tarot.* Newburyport USA, Weiser.

Gladwell, M. (2002). *The Tipping Point.* Back Bay Books, New York.

Govinda, L. A. (1966). *The Way of the White Clouds*.
Random House, London.

Graves, C. (2002). *Levels of Human Existence (Seminar 1971)*.
Santa Barbara, ECLET.

Griffith, J. (2011). *What is the Meaning of Life?*
In The Book of Real Answers to Everything!
From worldtransformation.com/what-is-the-meaning-of-life/

Grof, S. (2012). *Healing our Deepest Wounds*.
Washington, Stream of Experience Productions.

Haramein, N. (2011). *Double Torus Figure*.
YouTube youtu.be/vYOIBtxxark

Hardy, C. (2008). *The Sacred Network*. Rochester, Inner Traditions.

Harvey, A. (1997). *The Essential Mystics*. New York, HarperOne.

Hawking, S. (2010). *The Grand Design*. New York City, Bantam Books.

Hickman J. & Taegel W. (2015). *Neuroscience and Eco-fields*.
Ubiquity University Wisdom School webinar series.

Hielkema J.B. et al (2003). *Aanvullend Archeologisch Onderzoek*
op terrein Caesthage te Culemborg. Groningen, ARC.

Hielkema J.B., Vanden Borre J. et al (2004).
Een archeologisch begeleiding op het kasteelterrein Caesthage
te Culemborg, gemeente Culemborg. Groningen, ARC.

Jahn, B. & Dunne B. (2005). *The Pear Proposition (DVD/CD)*. Oakland, StripMindMedia.

Jahn, B. & Dunne B. (2015). *Molecular Memories*. Princeton, ICRL Press.

Johnson, K. (1997). *Jaguar Wisdom*. St. Paul Minnesota, Llewellyn Publications.

Jung, C.G. (1995). *Memories, Dreams, Reflections*. London: Fontana Press.

Kabbal, J. (2006). *Finding Clarity*. Berkeley, North Atlantic Books.

Keen, L. (1998). *Intuition Magic*. Charlottesville, Hampton Roads.

Kernaghan, E. (1995). *The Nameless Religion*. Paper found at raynemaker.com/namelessreligionHimalayas.pdf

Kieft, H. (2005) *Quantum Agriculture, Bridging frontline physics and intuitive knowledge of nature* http://www.movingworldviews.net/ Downloads/Papers/Kieft.pdf

Kingsley, P. (2010). *A Story Waiting to Pierce You*. Point Reyes, The Golden Sufi Center.

Kubler-Ross, E. (1997). *Living with Death and Dying*. New York, Scribner.

Lao Tzu (1999). *Tao Te Ching*. (Mitchell, S, Trans.). London, Frances Lincoln Limited.

Laszlo, E. (1994). *The Choice: evolution or extinction?*
Los Angeles, Tarcher.

Laszlo, E. (2001) *Macroshift: Navigating the Transformation to a Sustainable World.* San Francisco, Berrett – Koehler.

Laszlo, E. (2004). *Science and the Akashic Field.*
Vermont, Inner Traditions.

Laszlo, E. & Currivan, J. (2008). *CosMos.* London, Hay House.

Leary, T. (1987). *Info-Psychology.* Los Angeles, New Falcon Press.

Lefferts, M. (2012). *Fundamentals of Cosmometry.*
Wisdom University Teleseries.

Lehnert, J. (2014, Jan 4). *Universo 1.0.* Retrieved from universaria.net.

Levine, P. (1997). *Waking the Tiger: Healing Trauma.*
Berkeley, North Atlantic Books.

Leviton, R. (2005). *Encyclopedia of Earth Myths.*
Charlottesville, Hampton Roads.

Leviton, R. (2007). *Welcome to your Designer Planet!* Lincoln, iUniverse.

Lippe, I. & Schouten, M. (2010). *Leven in Verbinding.*
Utrecht, Ankh Hermes.

Lovelock, J. (2006). *Gaia's Revenge.* London, Allen Lane.

Lynas, M. (2007). *Six Degrees.* London, Fourth Estate .

Macy, J. (1998). *Coming Back to Life.* New Society Publishers.

Mahulikar, S.P. & Herwig, H.: (2009) *"Exact thermodynamic principles for dynamic order existence and evolution in chaos",* Chaos, Solitons & Fractals, v. 41(4), p1939-1948.

McTaggart, L. (2001). *The Field.* London, HarperCollins.

McTaggart, L. (2011). *The Bond: Connecting Through the Space Between Us.* Simon and Schuster.

Meijer & Geesink (2016). *Phonon Guided Biology: Architecture of Life and Conscious Perception are mediated by Toroidal Coupling of Phonon, Photon and Electron Information Fluxes at Eigen-frequencies.* NeuroQuantology, December 2016.

Melchizedek, D. (1990). *The Ancient Secret of the Flower of Life.* Flagstaff, Light Technology Publishing.

Merry, P. (2009). *Evolutionary Leadership.*
Pacific Grove, Integral Publishers.

Merry, P. (2011a). *Turquoise Research Project Phase 1 Report.* Utrecht, CHE NL School of Synnervation.

Merry, P. (2011b). *Of Dragons, Angels and Umbilici.* Retrieved from petermerry.org/blog/2011/of-dragons-angels-and-umbilici/.

Merry, P. (2012a). *From Evolution-Involution to Volution.*

Post-paper Cosmometry Course, Wisdom University.

Merry, P. (2012b). *Living in Mastery.*
Post-paper Living in Mastery Course, Wisdom University.

Merry, P. (2012c). *Sacred Leadership – Resilient Community; the energetics of transition.* Post-paper Sacred Leadership course, Wisdom University.

Morton C. & Thomas C.L. (1997). *The Mystery of the Crystal Skulls.* London, Element..

Nefiodow, L. & S. (2014). *The Sixth Kondratieff.*
Seattle, CreateSpace Independent Publishing Platform.

Nichol, L. Ed (2003). *The Essential David Bohm.* New York, Routledge

Patinkas (2014). *The Merkaba, Platonic Solids and Sacred Geometry.*
Retrieved from patinkas.co.uk/Merkaba_Feature_Article/merkaba_feature_article.html.

Pinchbeck, D. (2007). *2012 the Return of Quetzalcoatl.*
New York, Penguin..

Radin, D. (2004). *Electrodermal Presentiments of Future Emotions.*
Journal of Scientific Exploration, Vol. 18, No. 2, pp. 253-273, 2004.

Radin, D. (2013). *Supernormal: Science, Yoga, and the Evidence for Extraordinary Psychic Abilities.* Deepak Chopra, New York.

Ray, P. (2001). *The Cultural Creatives.* Broadway Books, Portland.

Rayne, C. (2005). *(Unpublished doctoral dissertation).*
Wisdom University, California.

Rayne, C. (2012). *Fundamentals of Energetics.*
Wisdom University intensive, Asheville NC .

Rees, P.A. (2013). *Involution. An Odyssey Reconciling Science to God.*
Stevenage, CollaborArt Books.

Rischard, J-F. (2002), *High Noon - 20 Global Problems,*
20 Years to Solve Them. Basic Books, New York.

Robertson, B. (2015). *Holacracy.* Henry Holt and Co., New York.

Roney-Dougal, S. (2010). *Where Science and Magic Meet.*
Glastonbury, Green Magic Publishing.

Ruggles, Clive L. N., ed. (2014). *The Handbook of Archaeoastronomy*
and Ethnoastronomy. New York, Springer.

Schneider, M. (1995). *A Beginner's Guide to Constructing the Universe.*
Harper Perennial, New York.

Senge, Jaworski, Scharmer and Flowers (2004). *Presence – Human*
Purpose and the Field of the Future. Cambridge (USA), SoL.

Sheldrake, R. (1981). *Morphic Resonance (4th Ed.).*
Vermont, Park Street Press.

Small Wright, M. (1997). *Co-Creative Science.* Warrenton, Perelandra Ltd.

Spangler, D. (2010). *Subtle Worlds.* Everett, Lorian Press.

Stewart, J. (2000). *Evolution's Arrow : The Direction of Evolution and the Future of Humanity.* Canberra, The Chapman Press.

Susskind, L. (1995). *The World as a Hologram.* Journal of Mathematical Physics 36 (11): 6377–6396.

Swimme, B. (1990). *Canticle to the Cosmos.* DVD.

Taegel, W. (2010). *The Sacred Council of Your Wild Heart.* Wimberley, 2nd Tier Publishing.

Taegel, W. (2012). *The Mother Tongue.* Wimberley, 2nd Tier Publishing.

Talbot, M. (1991). *The Holographic Universe.* London, HarperCollins Publishers.

Taylor, E. (2010). *Mind Programming.* Carlsbad, Hay House.

The Resonance Project (2011, June 16). *Power of Spin (Part 1).* Retrieved from youtu.be/tu62gxrZm0g.

The Three Initiates (2006). *The Kybalion.* UK, Filiquarian Publishing, LLC.

University of Southampton (2017). *Study reveals substantial evidence of holographic Universe.* Retrieved from m.phys.org/news/2017-01-reveals-substantial-evidence-holographic-Universe.html.

Van Daniken, E. (1969). *Waren de goden kosmonauten?*
Deventer, Uitgeverij N. Kluwer.

Watson, A. and Keating, D. 1999. *Architecture and sound:*
an acoustic analysis of megalithic monuments in prehistoric Britain.
Antiquity 73, p325-336.

Wheatley, M. (1999). *Leadership and the New Science.*
San Francisco, CA, Berrett-Koehler.

Whitehead, A. (1957). *Process and Reality.* New York, Macmillan.

Wilber, K. (1982). T*he Holographic Paradigm and Other Paradoxes.*
Boston, Shambhala Publications.

Wilber, K. (1995). *Sex, Ecology and Spirituality.*
Boston, Shambhala Publications.

Wilber, K. (1996). *Up from Eden.* Wheaton, Quest Books.

Wilber, K. (2000). *Integral Psychology.* Boston, Shambhala Publications.

Wilber, K. (2001). *A Theory of Everything.* Dublin, Gateway.

Wilber, K. (2003). *Boomeritis.* Boston, Shambhala.

Yoke (1997). *Atlantis.* Leusden, Uitgeverij Inzicht.

Young, A.M. (2015). *The Reflexive Universe.* Cambria USA,
Anodos Foundation.

Zukav, G. (1979). *The Dancing Wu Li Masters.* New York, Bantam.

www.ingramcontent.com/pod-product-compliance
Lightning Source LLC
Chambersburg PA
CBHW051301120626
46547CB00015B/2043